How to Become an Author

A Practical Guide

How to Become an Author

A Practical Guide

by

Arnold Bennett

GYAN

Published by

Gyan Publishing House
5, Ansari Road
Daryaganj, New Delhi-110002
Phone: 011-47034999, 9811692060
E-mail: books@gyanbooks.com

Distribution Network
gyanbooks.com
India, USA, Canada, UK, Australia, France

ISBN : 978-81-212-6170-8 (PB)
First Published, 1903

2nd Impression 2021

Printed at: Gyan Press, Delhi.

How to Become an Author
Author: Arnold Bennett

BY THE SAME AUTHOR

A MAN FROM THE NORTH

JOURNALISM FOR WOMEN

POLITE FARCES

FAME AND FICTION

THE GRAND BABYLON HOTEL

ANNA OF THE FIVE TOWNS

THE GATES OF WRATH

How to Become an Author

A Practical Guide

By

Arnold Bennett

Author of "Journalism for Women"
etc. etc.

Contents

CHAPTER I

THE LITERARY CAREER

How to Become an Author

CHAPTER I

THE LITERARY CAREER

Divisions of Literature.

In the year 1902 there were published 1743 volumes of fiction, 504 educational works, 480 historical and biographical works, 567 volumes of theology and sermons, 463 political and economical works, and 227 books of criticism and *belles-lettres*. These were the principal divisions of the grand army of 5839 new books issued during the year, and it will be seen that fiction is handsomely entitled to the first place. And the position of fiction is even loftier than appears from the above figures; for, with the exception of a few school-books which enjoy a popularity far exceeding all other popularities, and a few theological works, no class of book can claim as high a circulation per volume as the novel. More writers are engaged in fiction than in any other branch of literature, and their remuneration is better and perhaps surer than can be obtained in other literary markets. In esteem, influence, renown, and notoriety the novelists are also paramount.

Therefore in the present volume it will be proper for me to deal chiefly with the art and craft of fiction. For practical purposes I shall simply cut the whole of literature into two parts, fictional and non-fictional; and under the latter head I shall perforce crowd together the sublime and reverend muses of poetry, history, biography, theology, economy—everything, in short, that is not prose-fiction, save only plays; having regard to the extraordinary financial and artistic condition of the British stage and the British playwright at the dawn of the twentieth century, I propose to discuss the great "How" of the drama in a separate chapter unrelated to the general scheme of the book. As for journalism, though a journalist is not usually held to rank as an author, it is a fact that very many, if not most, authors begin by being journalists. Accordingly I shall begin with the subject of journalism.

Two Branches of Journalism: The Mechanical.

There are two branches of journalism, and it is necessary to distinguish sharply between them. They may be called the literary branch and the mechanical branch. To take the latter first, it is mainly the concern of reporters, of all sorts, and of sub-editors. It is that part of the executive side of journalism which can be carried out with the least expenditure of original brain-power. It consists in reporting —parliament, fashionable weddings, cricket-matches, company meetings, fat-stock shows; and in work of a sub-editorial character—proof-correcting, marshalling and co-ordinating the various items of an issue, cutting or lengthening articles according to need, modifying the tone of articles to coincide with the policy of the paper, and generally seeing that the editor and his brilliant original contributors do not, in the carelessness of genius, make fools of themselves. The sub-editor and the reporter, by reason of highly-developed natural qualifications, sometimes reach a wonderful degree of capacity for their duties, and the sub-editorial chair is often occupied by an individual who obviously has not the slightest intention of remaining in it. But, as a rule, the sub-editor and the reporter are mild and minor personages. Any man of average intelligence can learn how to report verbatim, how to write correct English, how to make incorrect English correct, how to describe neatly and tersely. Sub-editors and reporters are not born; they become so because their fathers or uncles were sub-editors or reporters, or by some other accident, not because instinct irresistibly carries them into the career; they would probably have succeeded equally well in another calling. They enter an office early, by a chance influence or by heredity, and they reach a status similar to that of a solicitor's managing-clerk. Fame is not for them, though occasionally they achieve a limited renown in professional circles. Their ultimate prospects are not glorious. Nor is their fiscal reward ever likely to be immense. In the provinces you may see the sub-editor or reporter of fifty who has reared a family on three pounds a week and will never earn three pounds ten. In London the very best mechanical posts yield as much as four hundred a year, and infrequently more; but the average salary of a thorough expert would decidedly not exceed two hundred and fifty, while the work performed is laborious, exacting, responsible, and often extremely inconvenient. Consider the case of the sub-editor of an evening paper, who must breakfast at 6 A.M. winter and summer, and of the sub-editor of a morning paper, who never gets to bed before three in the morning. Relatively, a clerk in a good house is better paid than a sub-editor or a reporter.

I shall have nothing more to say about this branch of journalism. Its duties are largely of an official kind and in the nature of routine, and are almost always studied practically in an office. A useful and trustworthy manual of them is Mr. John B. Mackie's *Modern Journalism: a Handbook of Instruction and Counsel for the Young Journalist*, published by Crosby, Lockwood & Son, price half-a-crown.

The Literary Branch.

I come now to the higher branch of journalism, that which is connected, more or less remotely, with literature. This branch merges with the lower branch in the person of the "descriptive-reporter," who may be a genius with the wages of an ambassador, like the late G. W. Steevens, or a mere hack who describes the Lord Mayor's procession and writes "stalwart emissaries of the law" when he means policemen. It includes, besides the aristocracy of descriptive reporting, reviewers, dramatic and other critics, financial experts, fashion-writers, paragraphists, miscellaneous contributors regular and irregular, assorted leader-writers, assistant editors, and editors;

I believe that newspaper proprietors also like to fancy themselves journalists. Very few ornaments of the creative branch of journalism become so by deliberate intention from the beginning. The average creative journalist enters his profession by "drifting" into it; the verb "to drift" is always used in this connection; the natural and proper assumption is that he was swept away on the flood of a powerful instinct. He makes a timid start by what is called "freelancing," that is, sending an unsolicited contribution to a paper in the hope that it will be accepted and paid for. He continues to shoot out unsolicited contributions in all directions until one is at length taken; then he thinks his fortune is made. In due course he gradually establishes a connection with one or more papers; perhaps he writes a book. On a day he suddenly perceives that an editor actually respects and relies on him; he is asked to "come into the office" sometimes, to do "things," and at last he gets the offer of an appointment. Lo! he is a full-fledged journalist; yet the intermediate stages leading from his first amateurish aspiring to his achieved position have been so slight, vague, and uncertain, that he can explain them neither to himself nor to others. He has "drifted into journalism." And let me say here that he has done the right thing. It is always better to enter a newspaper office from towards the top than from towards the bottom. It is, in my opinion, an error of tactics for a youth with a marked bent towards journalism, to join a staff at an early age as a proof-reader, reporter, or assistant sub-editor; he is apt to sink into a groove, to be obsessed by the routine instead of the romance of journalism, and to lose intellectual elasticity.

The creative branch of journalism is proportionately no better paid than the mechanical branch. The highest journalistic post in the kingdom is reputed to be worth three thousand a year, an income at which scores of lawyers, grocers, bishops, music-hall artistes, and novelists would turn up their noses. A thousand a year is a handsome salary for the editor of a first-class organ; some editors of first-class organs receive much less, few receive more. (The London County Council employs eleven officers at a salary of over a thousand a year each, and five at a thousand each.) An assistant editor is worth something less than half an editor, while an advertisement manager is worth an editor and an assistant editor added together. A leader-writer may receive from four hundred to a thousand a year. No man can earn an adequate livelihood as a book-reviewer or a dramatic or musical critic, pure and simple; but a few women by much industry contrive to flourish by fashion-writing alone. The life of a man without a regular appointment who exists as a freelance may be adventurous, but it is scarcely worth living. The rate of pay for journalistic contributions varies from seven and sixpence to two guineas per thousand words; the average is probably under a pound; not a dozen men in London get more than two guineas a thousand for unsigned irregular contributions. A journalist at once brilliant, reliable, industrious, and enterprising, may be absolutely sure of a reasonably good income, provided he keeps clear of editorships and does not identify himself too prominently with any single paper. If he commits either of these indiscretions, his welfare largely depends on the unwillingness of his proprietor to sell his paper. A change of proprietorship usually means a change of editors and of prominent contributors, and there are few more pathetic sights in Fleet Street than the Famous Journalist dismissed through no fault of his own.

On the whole, it cannot be made too clear that journalism is never a gold-mine except for newspaper proprietors, and not always for them. The journalist sells his brains in a weak market. Other things being equal, he receives decidedly less than he would receive in any pursuit save those of the graphic arts, sculpture, and music. He must console himself by meditating upon the romance, the publicity, and the influential character of his profession. Whether these intangible things are a sufficient consolation to the able, conscientious man who gives his best for, say, three or four hundred a year and the prospect of a precarious old age, is a question happily beyond the scope of my treatise.

Fiction.

I have made no mention of the natural gifts of universal curiosity, alertness, inextinguishable verve, and vivacious style which are necessary to success in creative journalism, because the aspirant will speedily discover by results whether or not he possesses them. If he fails in the earlier efforts of freelancing, he will learn thereby that he is not a born journalist, and the "drifting" process will automatically cease. For the same reason I need not enter upon an academic discussion of the qualifications proper to a novelist. In practice, nobody plunges blindly into the career of fiction. Long before the would-be novelist has reached the point at which to turn back means ignominious disaster, he will have ascertained with some exactness the exchange value of his qualifications, and will have set his course accordingly. There is the rare case of the beginner who achieves popularity by his first book. This apparently fortunate person will be courted by publishers and flattered by critics, and in the ecstasy of a facile triumph he may be tempted to abandon a sure livelihood "in order to devote himself entirely to fiction." One sees the phrase occasionally in literary gossip. The temptation should be resisted at all costs. A slowly-built reputation as a novelist is nearly indestructible; neither time nor decay of talent nor sheer carelessness will quite kill it; your Mudie subscriber, once well won, is the most faithful adherent in the world. But the reputation that springs up like a mushroom is apt to fade like a mushroom; modern instances might easily be cited, and will occur to the student of publishers' lists. Moreover, it is unquestionable that many writers can produce one striking book and no more. Therefore the beginner in fiction should not allow himself to be dazzled by the success of a first book.

The success of a seventh book is a sufficient assurance for the future, but the success of a first book should be followed by the success of two others before the author ventures, in Scott's phrase, to use fiction as a crutch and not merely as a stick.

Speaking broadly, fiction is a lucrative profession; it cannot compare with stock-broking, or brewing, or practice at the parliamentary bar, but it is tolerably lucrative. Never before, despite the abolition of the three-volume novel, did so many average painstaking novelists earn such respectable incomes as at the present day. And the rewards of the really successful novelist seem to increase year by year. A common course is to begin with short stories for magazines and weeklies. These vary in length from two to six thousand words, and the payment, for unknown authors, varies from half a guinea to three guineas per thousand. The leading English magazines willingly pay fifteen guineas for a five-thousand-word story. But to make a living out of short stories alone is impossible in England. I believe it may be accomplished in America, where at least one magazine is prepared to pay forty dollars per thousand words irrespective of the author's reputation.

The production of sensational serials is remunerative up to a certain point. The halfpenny dailies and the popular penny weeklies will pay from ten shillings to thirty shillings per thousand words; and the newspaper syndicates, who buy to sell again to a number of clients simultaneously, sometimes go as far as two pounds per thousand for an author who has little reputation but who suits them. Thus a man may make a hundred pounds by working hard for a month, with the chance of an extra fifty pounds for book-rights afterwards. A writer who makes a name as a sensational serialist does not often get beyond three pounds per thousand, though the syndicates may be more generous, rising to five or six pounds per thousand. I should doubt whether even the most popular of sensational serialists can obtain more than six pounds per thousand. In this particular market a reputation is less valuable than elsewhere. And it must also be remembered that the sale of sensational serials in book form is seldom remarkable.

The mild domestic novelist who plods steadily along, and whose work is suitable for serial issue, is in a better position than the mere sensation-monger. She—it is often a "she"—may get from three to six pounds per thousand for serial rights as her reputation waxes, and her book-rights may be anything from two hundred to a thousand pounds. I can state with certainty that it is not unusual for a novelist who has never really had an undubitable success, but who has built up a sort of furtive half-reputation, to make a thousand pounds out of a novel, first and last. Such a person can write two novels a year with ease. I have more than once been astonished at the sums received by novelists whom, both in an artistic and a commercial sense, I had regarded as nobodies. I know an instance of a particularly mild and modest novelist who was selling the book-rights of her novels outright for three hundred pounds apiece. One day it occurred to her to demand double that sum, and to her immense surprise the publisher immediately accepted the suggestion. I should estimate that this author can comfortably write a book in three months.

The Really Successful Novelist.

The novelist who once really gets himself talked about, or, in other words, sells at least ten thousand copies of a book, and who is capable of living up to his reputation, soon finds that he is on a bed of roses. For serial rights in England and America he may get fifteen pounds per thousand, making twelve hundred pounds for an eighty-thousand-word novel. For book-rights he will be paid at the rate of about seventy-five pounds per thousand copies of the circulation; so that if his book sells ten thousand copies in England and five thousand copies in America, he receives eleven hundred and twenty-five pounds. Baron Tauchnitz will give from twenty-five to fifty pounds for the continental rights, and the colonial rights are worth something. The grand total for the book will thus be quite two thousand four hundred pounds. This novelist will probably produce three novels in two years. Magazines will pay sixty pounds apiece and upwards for his short stories, and from time to time the stories will be collected and issued in a volume which is good for a few hundred pounds. By writing a hundred and fifty thousand words a year he will make an annual income of three thousand five hundred pounds. His habit will be to write a thousand words a day three days a week, and on each working day he will earn about twenty-five pounds. All which is highly agreeable—but then the man is highly exceptional.

The case of the novelist who has a vogue of the most popular kind, that is to say, whose books reach a circulation of from fifty to a hundred thousand copies, is even more opulent, luxurious, and lofty. The sale of a hundred thousand copies of a six-shilling novel means that the author receives upwards of seven thousand five hundred pounds. The value of the serial rights of a book by such an author is extremely high in many cases, though sometimes it is nothing. There are ten authors in England who can count on receiving at least four thousand pounds for any long novel they choose to write, and there are several who have made, and may again make, twenty thousand pounds from a single book, which is at the rate of about four shillings a word. And seeing that any author who knows his craft can easily —despite statements to the contrary in illustrated interviews and other grandiose manifestations of bombast—compose three thousand words of his very best in a week, the pecuniary rewards of the first-class "boom" should satisfy the most avaricious and exacting.

The Sagacious Mediocrity.

But the average mediocre novelist, too good to excite a mob to admiration, and not good enough to be taken seriously by persons of taste, can have only a polite interest in the foregoing statistics. It remains for me to assure the average mediocre novelist *in posse*, that, if he minds his task, produces regularly, perseveres in one vein, judiciously compromises between his own ideals and the desires of the public, and conscientiously puts his best workmanship into all he does, he may safely rely on a reasonable return in coin. There are scores of mediocrities who make upwards of five hundred a year from fiction by labour that cannot be called fatiguing, writers who never accomplish anything worthy of the name of art, but who fulfil a harmless and perhaps useful function in our effete civilisation. The novelist, even the mediocrity, works under felicitous conditions. He is tied to no place and no times. He probably writes for three hours a day, five days a week, nine months in the year. He can produce his tale beneath an Italian sky as easily as in the groves of Brixton or Hampstead. No man is his master, and he is dependent on nobody's goodwill and on nobody's whim. Only three things can seriously hurt him: a grave failure of health, a European war, and a prolonged strike of bookbinders. The efflux of time will serve but to solidify his reputation, if he uses it well; his income will rise for years, and will remain stable for more years, and though ultimately it must fall it will not fall as fast as once it rose. On the other hand, the novelist who will not study his readers, who presumes on their obtuseness to offer them less than his best, and who lacks stedfastness, may confidently anticipate a decreasing income, no matter what his powers.

Non-Fictional Writing.

The well-known division of authors into those who want to write because they have something to say, and those who merely want to write, is peculiarly applicable to the non-fictional field. To the former class belong the authors of the best histories, biographies, travel books, theological books, and scientific, critical, and technical treatises. The latter class is composed of a heterogeneous crowd of compilers, rearrangers, and general literary middlemen anxious to turn an honest penny. The former class seldom needs advice of an expert nature, for the troubling consciousness of a "message" almost invariably connotes the ability to deliver that message with all needful lucidity and conviction; no one is so sure of achieving the aims of the literary craftsman as the man who has something to say and wishes to say it simply and have done with it. The latter class needs direction, for it has none of its own; and its principal desire is to make money, whereas with the former class the financial side of the work is usually secondary. Many great works of fiction have been accomplished because the authors wanted money, and wanted it badly and in large quantities, but this can be said of extremely few great non-fictional works.

The literary aspirant who merely wants to write, and who cannot write fiction, will have to be content with the prospect of a smaller income than he could derive from the imaginative gift did he possess it. But nevertheless, with ingenuity, he can make money. Popular biographies—especially of princes, artists, and scoundrels, anecdotic histories of places, people, and pastimes—especially of pastimes, smeltings of the ore of antique magazines, diaries, and other records, guides to everything past, present, and to come, and descriptions of travel undertaken in order to be described—the field open to the activities of the ingenious hack is well-nigh boundless; in my opinion it is yet far from being fully exploited. The demand for the Anecdote glorified in cloth covers is prodigious and insatiable, and if the reward of the anecdote is not overpowering, neither is the uncreative labour of serving it up. Among the most remunerative forms of non-fictional writing is the "gossipy" book dealing lightly with a past epoch, not too remote. A well contrived chitchat on the Reign of Terror, or the Age of Johnson, or the Regency, garnished with reproductions of a few old prints, is always welcomed by the libraries. Such volumes are put forth in imposing ornamental exteriors at a fairly high price, and a twenty per cent. royalty on them means a satisfactory result to the author. It is not uncommon for Mudies alone to buy two hundred copies of a half-guinea, sixteen-shilling, or guinea book of glorified anecdote. Taking the lowest price, and assuming that a thousand copies are sold, the return to the ingenious compiler is a hundred pounds. The profits are frequently more, and not often less. The popular biography and the popular monograph do not, I am afraid, pay quite so well, because publishers have a preference for buying them from the author outright at a rate which probably does not average more than one pound per thousand words. But even this is not precisely despicable when one considers that the only qualifications necessary to the anecdotist and the compiler are a brisk, clear style and some skill in the arrangement of material.

The subject of popular non-fictional writing for money is so wide and various that it is impossible to select for discussion any career that would be fairly typical. The success of the book-concocter (I use the term without disrespect) depends on his invention and versatility, and his aptitude to foresee the changes of public taste. At best he is not likely to acquire riches ; but, provided always that he has access to a great library, he may materially add to his income by intermittently concocting. He should not depend wholly on this branch of literature for a livelihood, although I admit that it might be possible, by using several pseudonyms and several publishers and an inordinate amount of research for topics, to earn as much in strenuous, tireless concoction as a second-rate novelist earns without undue exertion.

CHAPTER II

THE FORMATION OF STYLE

CHAPTER II

THE FORMATION OF STYLE

An Art of Words.

Literature is the art of using words. This is not a platitude, but a truth of the first importance, a truth so profound that many writers never get down to it, and so subtle that many other writers who think they see it never in fact really comprehend it. The business of the author is with words. The practisers of other arts, such as music and painting, deal with ideas and emotions, but only the author has to deal with them by means of words. Words are his exclusive possession among creative artists and craftsmen. They are his raw material, his tools and instruments, his manufactured product, his Alpha and Omega. He may abound in ideas and emotions of the finest kind, but those ideas and emotions cannot be said to have an effective existence until they are expressed; they are limited to the extent of their expression; and their expression is limited to the extent of the author's skill in the use of words. I smile when I hear people say, "If I could *write*, if I could only put down what I feel—!" Such people beg the whole question. The ability to *write* is the sole thing peculiar to literature—not the ability to think nor the ability to feel, but the ability to write, to utilise words. The skill to write is far less common than the skill to think and feel. The author cannot demand of the reader that he shall penetrate beyond the meaning of the written word and perceive that which the author wished to convey, but which lack of skill prevented him from conveying. And even if the author were entitled to demand such a feat from the reader, the reader could not perform it. Nothing is less possible than that a reader should be capable of doing for the author what the author has been incapable of doing for himself. I particularly desire the literary aspirant to meditate long and seriously upon this section, for it is the most vital in the book, and the most likely to be overlooked and forgotten.

If literary aspirants genuinely felt that literature was the art of using words, bad, slipshod writing—writing that stultifies the thought and emotion which it is designed to render effective—would soon be a thing of the past. For they would begin at the beginning, as apprentices to all other arts are compelled to do. The serious student of painting who began his apprenticeship by trying to paint a family group, would be regarded as a lunatic. But the literary aspirant who begins with a novel is precisely that sort of lunatic, and the fact that he sometimes gets himself into print does not in the least mitigate his lunacy. The student of painting would be instructed to copy drawings, to draw from the antique, to draw from the single model, to accustom himself to the medium of oils, before he made any attempt at a composition in oil-painting. In other words, he would be told to begin at the beginning. And this is what the literary aspirant must do. I am perfectly aware that literature is by tradition loose and unsystematised in comparison with other arts. I am perfectly aware that many authors have in a manner "succeeded," who obviously did not begin at the beginning and never had the sense to go back to the beginning. Nevertheless, I assert that it pays to begin at the beginning. There is not a successful inexpert author writing to-day who would not be more successful—who would not be better esteemed and in receipt of a larger income—if he had taken the trouble to become expert. Skill does count; skill is always worth its cost in time and labour.

The Self-Education of the Aspirant.

Every aspirant should pursue the following course:—

He should learn to spell. Spelling is the first thing in the craft of literature. Most people imagine that they can spell correctly; but the simple accomplishment is extremely rare. You who read this imagine that you can spell correctly. But hand a dictionary to a friend and ask him to test you in common words, and the chances are that you will be undeceived in five minutes. It is a fact that not one person in ten can be relied on to spell quite ordinary words correctly, and I do not believe that writers are superior to their fellows in the matter of orthography. The aspirant should have ten minutes' practice in spelling every day. Some vain and pig-headed aspirant, afraid of being mistaken for a schoolboy, will think that this counsel is ridiculous. It is not ridiculous, but intensely practical.

He should study the etymology of words. No writer who has not a sound acquaintance with the history of words can possibly make full use of his powers. A first-class dictionary is essential. There are several in the market. The best is, of course, the *New English Dictionary.* It is still far from completion, and its price is rather high; but it is worth its price to any writer. The *Century Dictionary* is perhaps the next best. The writer should also have a small exclusively etymological dictionary. Skeat's *Concise Etymological Dictionary*, published by the Clarendon Press, 5s. 6d., is the best; but Chambers' little *Etymological Dictionary*, 3s. 6d., is not to be despised. These dictionaries should be read daily. I have been told by one of our greatest living novelists, that he constantly reads the dictionary, and that in his youth he read the dictionary through several times. I may recount the anecdote of Buckle, the historian of civilisation, who, when a certain dictionary was mentioned in terms of praise, said: "Yes, it is one of the few dictionaries I have read through with pleasure." Dictionaries should surely be interesting to him who is interested in words, and the first characteristic of the born writer is that he is interested in words.

But no dictionary can pretend to be exhaustive in its treatment of any word; it cannot, for instance, follow a word into its combinations with other words; and it must necessarily leave much to the deductive powers of the student. Therefore the aspirant must pursue his inquiries into words beyond the covers of dictionaries. He must study words in English literature itself. And in order to learn the method of such study, he should read a book like the late Archbishop Trench's *On the Study of Words*, published by Messrs. Kegan Paul, and now approaching its thirtieth edition. In the light of recent etymological research, Trench is admittedly inaccurate, but the spirit and the method in and by which he approaches and grasps his subject are admirable. His enthusiasm is as infectious as a cold which runs through a household. A later, more elaborate, and more accurate book is *Words and their Ways in English Speech*, by two American professors, J. B. Greenhough and G. L. Kittredge, published by Messrs. Macmillan: a simply delightful volume, which it is the duty of every literary aspirant to read, and to read again. The intimacy with words which must infallibly result from such study as I here indicate, will have its immediate result in an improvement—an increased vigour, picturesqueness, subtlety, and adroitness—of the aspirant's style. And let the worldly-minded remember that these qualities of vigour, picturesqueness, subtlety, and adroitness, ultimately stand for pounds per thousand.

The aspirant should study English grammar, a subject seldom treated with any glimmering of sense in high-schools, but one which a board school teacher may be trusted to teach satisfactorily. It is obviously a truism that the man who does not understand the grammatical principles which underlie the construction of English sentences, cannot rely on his ability to construct a sentence correctly. Yet how few writers, especially women-writers, are capable of "parsing" and "analysing" the sentences which they so cheerfully put together! The two manuals which I recommend in this connection are Dr. Richard Morris's *Primer of English Grammar* and Mr. John Wetherell's *Exercises on Morris's*

English Grammar (both published by Messrs. Macmillan at a shilling each). They can be thoroughly mastered in quite a short time, with or without the assistance of a teacher. Again I must warn the aspirant not to scorn these beginnings of the great art of literature. It is always to the profit of a craftsman to "know his business," and the writer who cannot with ease and assurance "parse" and "analyse," emphatically does not know his business.

Writing.

The aspirant should study English composition. This advice may seem unnecessary, but many writers never study composition. They write—and trust in Heaven to save them from doing anything absolutely fatuous. They have no notion of the canons of composition. They commit literary sins against good form so atrocious that social sins of the same heinousness would banish them from the dinner-tables of decently-bred people. These writers abound, and their existence is a blot on English letters. No one can write correctly without deliberately and laboriously learning how to write correctly. On the other hand, every one can learn to write correctly who takes sufficient trouble. Correct writing is a mechanical accomplishment; it could be acquired by a stockbroker. The best book on the subject is Professor John Nichol's *English Composition*, published by Messrs. Macmillan at a shilling. The companion volume, *Questions and Exercises on English Composition*, same publishers and price, should also be obtained. Professor Nichol deals with punctuation, but many students will be glad to have *Stops; or, How to Punctuate*, by Mr. Paul Allardyce, published by Mr. Fisher Unwin. In these quite small books the aspirant may gather all the technical information necessary to good composition, from the use of a comma to the placing of a participial phrase in a complex sentence, from the avoidance of solecisms to the proper management of similes and metaphors.

So guided, the aspirant should regularly

practise writing. He must write for the sake of writing. He should write from five hundred to a thousand words a day, according to his leisure and facility. As an athlete trains, as an acrobat painfully tumbles in private, so must the literary aspirant write. I do not much care what he writes about, at the commencement, if only he writes enough; but the better his subjects the more useful and the more interesting will be his practice. He may try to report conversations (an excellent device), or to describe episodes, scenes, and persons. Or he may compose essays, articles, or short stories, "not necessarily with a view to publication, but as a guarantee of good faith." The one paramount rule is that he must always write his best; he must never leave a sentence until he is convinced that he cannot improve it. Any lack of conscientious endeavour after the best will vitiate the most regular and persistent practice. Everything written should be read aloud, if possible to another person—not immediately, but after an interval of several days. The test of reading aloud is a severe one — perhaps the most severe test to which literature can be put— and it will certainly disclose errors, weaknesses, and crudities that might otherwise have escaped attention; it is particularly valuable as an aid to the decision of questions of punctuation, for where the voice of the reader pauses, there ought the comma to be.

Concurrently with his writing, the aspirant must read and study good models. I need not give a list of good models, since every one is acquainted with the names of the masterpieces of English literature. The important thing is that the aspirant should study most those masterpieces which most strongly appeal to him. If Thackeray, or Stevenson, or Sir Thomas Browne, or Charles Lamb specially attract him, let him, in the early stages, imitate Thackeray, Stevenson, Browne, or Lamb. Let him deliberately imitate them; the act will help him in the end to arrive at his own originality. He may even go so far as to paraphrase, from memory, the favourite passages of his favourite authors;

the subsequent comparison of the paraphrase with the exemplar will be an education for him.

Two Difficulties.

There are two principal difficulties which beset the path of the beginner in composition. The first difficulty is the smallness of his vocabulary. He cannot express his meaning with exactitude, because at the moment of writing he cannot think of the precise word needed; he may be acquainted with the word, but it refuses to occur to him. Reading, including the perusal of dictionaries, will gradually conquer this difficulty. A more instant palliative of it is that wonderful collection of synonyms, Roget's *Thesaurus of English Words and Phrases, Classified and Arranged so as to Facilitate the Expression of Ideas and Assist in Literary Composition*, published by Messrs. Longman at half a guinea. Every writer should possess this volume, which by its ingenious index will enable him to recover any lost word, and by presenting him with a complete series of words relating to any given idea will help him to a final nicety of expression. I sang the virtues of Roget with some enthusiasm in my book *Journalism for Women*, and a leader-writer in the *Daily News* censured my song. An indiscreet use of Roget may, I admit, lead to verbosity and other affectations; but all indiscretions lead to mischief. My opinion that Roget's *Thesaurus* is the most useful of all mechanical aids to good writing remains unchanged. I have seen the tattered tome on the desks of some of the most distinguished authors in England, and, for myself, nothing would induce me to part with my Roget except the publication of a revised and enlarged edition of him.

The second and more serious difficulty is the instinctive tendency of the young author to compose in phrases instead of in single words. In accounting for the tediousness of second-rate authors, Schopenhauer said that owing to their lack of clearly defined thought, their writing was "an indefinite, obscure interweaving of words, current phrases, worn-out terms of speech, and fashionable expressions."

And he added: "It is only *intelligent* writers who place individual words together with a full consciousness of their use, and select them with deliberation." This sentence is the utterance of practical wisdom. The first sign of unintelligent writing, the first cause of tediousness, is the presence of ready-made, trite phrases. From an entirely respectable book, by an author of repute, which has just passed through my hands, I cull at random a handful of these phrases: Joined the majority [for "died"], strong-minded female, needless to say, *terra firma*, fondly imagined, absolutely non-plussed, deaf old party, respect due to the cloth, beat a hasty retreat, called into requisition, graciously volunteered, *par excellence.* Now it is obvious that this author was content largely to use second-hand, worn-out material for the expression of his ideas; that even if his ideas were originally distinct, they must have lost much of their distinctness in being thus forced into an old mould.

Avoid the use of ready-made phrases.

When they present themselves, as they will do, reject them. Define your thought clearly, and you will discover that its expression demands a new phrase, invented word by word specially for it. Your business is to invent that phrase, simply and naturally. Besides leading to dulness and banality, the use of trite proverbial phrases leads also to exaggeration and misstatement. When Boswell told Johnson of the earthquake shock at Leek, Johnson remarked: "Sir, it will be much exaggerated in public talk: for, in the first place, the common people do not accurately adapt their thoughts to the objects; nor, secondly, do they accurately adapt their words to their thoughts: they do not mean to lie; but, taking no pains to be exact, they give you very false accounts. A great part of their language is proverbial. If anything rocks at all, they say *it rocks like a cradle;* and in this way they go on." And in this way the careless, unintelligent author goes on, too.

When a sentence has been written, every

word in it should be interrogated *separately*, and made to justify the position which it occupies.

Style.

Having disposed of the lower aspects, the more mechanical details, of composition, I am free to approach the great and deeply misunderstood question of "style."

Most persons, including many literary beginners, have an entirely wrong notion of the significance of the phrase, "literary style." They imagine that it necessarily includes the idea of pomp, statelinesss, magnificence, lyricism, richness, elaboration; that it is something beyond, and in addition to, accurate, lucid description. Here I will print a specimen of English :—

"He who has once stood beside the grave, to look back upon the companionship which has been for ever closed, feeling how impotent *there* are the wild love and the keen sorrow, to give one instant's pleasure to the pulseless heart, or atone in the lowest measure to the departed spirit for the hour of unkindness, will scarcely for the future incur that debt to the heart, which can only be discharged to the dust. But the lesson which men receive as individuals, they do not learn as nations. Again and again they have seen their noblest descend into the grave, and have thought it enough to garland the tombstone when they had not crowned the brow, and to pay the honour to the ashes which they had denied to the spirit. Let it not displease them that they are bidden, amidst the tumult and the dazzle of their busy life, to listen for the few voices, and watch for the few lamps, which God has tuned and lighted to charm and to guide them, that they may not learn their sweetness by their silence, nor their light by their decay."

This passage has the qualities which for most people constitute a good literary style. Let me now give another specimen of English :—

"The following occurrence ought not to be passed over in silence, in a place where so few notable ones are to be met with. Last Wednesday night, while we were at supper, between the hours of eight and nine, I heard an unusual noise in the back parlour, as if one of the hares was entangled, and endeavouring to disengage herself. I was just going to rise from the table when it ceased. In about five minutes a voice on the outside of the parlour door inquired if one of my hares had got away. I immediately rushed into the next room, and found that my poor favourite Puss had made her escape. She had gnawed in sunder the strings of the lattice-work, with which I thought I had sufficiently secured the window, and which I preferred to any other sort of blind, because it admitted plenty of air. From thence I hastened to the kitchen, where I saw the redoubtable Thomas Freeman, who told me, that having seen her, just after she had dropped into the street, he attempted to cover her with his hat, but she screamed out and leaped directly over his head. I then desired him to pursue as fast as possible, and added Richard Coleman to the chase, as being nimbler, and carrying less weight than Thomas; not expecting to see her again, but desirous to learn, if possible, what became of her. In something less than an hour Richard returned, almost breathless, with the following account: That soon after he began to run he left Tom behind him, and came in sight of a most numerous hunt of men, women, children, and dogs; that he did his best to keep back the dogs, and presently outstripped the crowd, so that the race was at last disputed between himself and Puss—she ran right through the town, and down the lane that leads to Dropshort. A little before she came to the house he got the start and turned her; she pushed for the town again, and soon after she entered it sought shelter in Mr. Wagstaff's tanyard, adjoining to old Mr. Drake's. Sturge's harvest men were at supper, and saw her from the opposite side of the way. There she encountered the tan-pits full of water; and while she was struggling out of one pit and plunging into another, and almost drowned, one of the men drew her out by the ears and secured her. She was then well washed in a bucket, to get the lime out of her coat, and brought home in a sack at ten o'clock. This frolic cost us four shillings. . . ."

The untrained taste will probably discover no distinction of style in this relation of a hare's escape. Nevertheless, the peroration of Ruskin's famous Introduction to *Modern Painters* is not more distinguished in its own way than Cowper's letter to the Rev. John Newton is distinguished in its own way. Each is fine literature. The aspirant, if he cannot feel the rightness of this judgment, must try to feel it until he succeeds in doing so.

Richness, elaboration, lyricism, and so forth, may be present in a particular good style, but they are not essential elements of good style in general. When a writer expresses his individuality and his mood with accuracy, lucidity, and sincerity, and with an absence of ugliness, then he achieves good style. Style—it cannot be too clearly understood—is not a certain splendid something which the writer adds to his meaning. It is *in* the meaning; it is that part of the meaning which specially reflects his individuality and his mood. When Stevenson wished to visualise calm sea-water on a clear night, he wrote the beautiful simple phrase, "star-reflecting harbours." When Kipling essayed the same feat he wrote the striking, aggressive, explosive phrase, "planet-powdered floors." Each expressed himself while expressing the idea. The whole difference between the individualities of Stevenson and Kipling can be discerned in the difference between those two phrases. Style is the result of self-expression, of the writer being himself. If a writer is individually distinguished, then, after he has learnt his craft, his style will be distinguished. If he is individually commonplace, then his style will be commonplace.

Being One's Self.

I have said that style is the result of the writer being himself. But every man is himself instinctively; he has not to take thought in order to be himself. Therefore the young writer should dismiss from his mind that abstract entity which he calls style. He should forget all about style. His sole aim should be to write down, accurately and lucidly and honestly, what he means, always trying to avoid positively ugliness, but not consciously aiming after positive beauty. Let him lose himself completely in the effort to express his meaning in the fewest and clearest words. Good style—beauty, charm, gaiety, splendour, stateliness—will come of itself, unasked and unperceived, so far as the natural distinction of his individuality permits. Good style is not a bird that can be brought down with a shot-gun.

Let me add that to be one's natural self is the most difficult thing in literature. To be one's natural self in a drawing-room full of observant eyes is scarcely the gift of the simple débutant, but rather of the experienced diner-out. So in literature: it is not the expert but the unpractised beginner who is guilty of artificiality. The chief end of the literary apprenticeship is to combine naturalness and sincerity with grace and force. Hence the aspirant must familiarise himself with the fundamental idea, at first perhaps strange and alarming, that the process which lies before him is not one of acquiring, but of stripping off.

There are many treatises on style. I shall recommend none of them, for the same reason that I would not recommend a book of "household medicine" to a hypochondriac. Let the aspirant read good stuff, learn the rules, and try to say merely what he means.

CHAPTER III

JOURNALISM

CHAPTER III

JOURNALISM

The Journalistic Attitude.

THE beginner who aspires to be an outside contributor, or—in the slang of the profession—a freelance, must first of all comprehend the journalistic attitude. The freelance, the sender-in of unsolicited contributions, offers his wares in a market to which he has not been invited, a market which in theory does not want him. He must therefore, if he hopes to do any business, devote all his efforts to finding out what the real needs of the market are. Now journalism, as practised to-day, is quite a modern invention. In the history of no art, perhaps, has there been a change so sudden and so fundamental as that which separates the journalism of twenty-five years ago from the journalism of the present time. Modern daily journalism was invented by Mr. W. T. Stead, on the *Pall Mall Gazette*, and further developed by Mr. T. P. O'Connor on the *Star*. After a short interval it was carried a step further by Mr. Alfred Harmsworth on the *Daily Mail*. These three men have been or are the great revolutionary forces in daily journalism. Their influence has affected all that branch of journalism, whether daily, weekly, or monthly, which deals with current events and leads or expresses public opinion. The other branch, that which has no "views" on anything, and merely seeks to entertain, owes its form to Sir George Newnes, who hit on the idea of *Tit-Bits*. Every characteristic of modern journalism can be traced back to one of the four papers I have mentioned. The *Daily Mail* was an ingenious and entirely logical combination of the other three, and its success has been the justification of the logic which evolved it.

The difference between the old and the new journalism is twofold, and lies partly in the journal's attitude to its readers, and partly in its attitude to the world. The old journalism said to itself, in effect, when it wrote its copy: "This is what our readers ought to like. This is good for them. This is genuinely important. This ought to interest. This cannot be omitted. This is our expert opinion on a vital affair—" And so on. The new journalism says to itself: "*Will* our readers like this, *will* they be interested in it? Let us not forget that our readers are ignorant, ill-informed, impatient under intellectual strain, and not anxiously concerned about many really vital matters. Let us remember that they live chiefly for themselves and for the moment; that in fact they are human. Let us look the situation in the face and decide whether our readers—*not as they ought to be, but as they actually are*—will read and be interested in this thing. If they won't, however excellent it may be, it is of no use to us." Again, the old journalism considered that many aspects of life were beneath its notice. The old journalism ignored nearly everything except politics, law, trade, and the arts. The new journalism ignores nothing, considers nothing beneath its notice. Everything that is human is good enough for the new journalism, and the more human it is, the more warmly does the new journalism welcome it.

The general effect of the new journalism is mixed. By sheer skill it has invested with interest a number of topics that once were hopelessly dull, and has thus brilliantly compelled the average man to acquire useful information and to form views on subjects which formerly he ignored. In short, it has educated the average man. On the other hand, its growing tendency to pander unduly to the prejudices and the intellectual laziness of the average man is thoroughly bad.

The business of the journalistic aspirant, however, is not to criticise tendencies but to follow them. And the freelance must do a little more than follow them; he must overtake them and pass them. The watch-words of modern journalism are Freshness, Brightness, and Human Interest. The efforts of the freelance, therefore, since they have to attract notice in a crowd, must be very fresh, very bright, very full of human interest.

The whole philosophy of the freelance can be summarised under three heads or maxims:—

(1) Not the sort of thing that I want to write, but the sort of thing that the public wants to read!

(2) Every department of life, no matter how apparently commonplace, has its interesting side. As a freelance it is my business to see that side and to utilise it.

(3) Every good new thing is saleable, but the proper market must be found for it.

The Sorts of Journals.

Let us imagine the journalistic aspirant standing in front of the bookstall at Charing Cross Station. He sees before him a very large representative selection of all branches of the English press, so large, indeed, and so various as to be extremely confusing and rather terrifying. The aspirant says to himself: "Most of these papers are prepared to buy contributions from outsiders. Probably most of the numbers actually on this stall contain unsolicited articles that were offered by freelances. I too wish to be a freelance, and to send in articles that will be accepted and paid for. How am I to begin?"

He must begin by classifying and studying the papers at a reading-room, and deciding which paper, or which kind of paper, he will first attack. His immediate aim in life is now to get an article into a paper. He must therefore sink all his own preferences, vanities, scruples, and prejudices, all his little notions about what the art of journalism ought to be, and deliberately practise the art of journalism as it is. He must be entirely worldly, entirely possessed by the idea of getting money in exchange for an article—not for the sake of the money, but because money is the sole proof of success in the enterprise. After he has made money he will have plenty of time in which to endeavour to improve the tone of journalism and preach his own particular fancies. As works of reference in this department, he should have either Sell's *Dictionary of the World's Press* (7s. 6d), or, more compact and compendious, Willing's *Press Guide* (1s.). These two volumes give all addresses, dates of publication, &c. *The Literary Year-Book* (published by Mr. George Allen, 3s. 6d.) gives some useful particulars as to the requirements and methods of certain monthly magazines, obtained direct from the editors.

The class of paper first to be mentioned is the popular penny weekly, of which the chief examples are *Tit-Bits*, *Pearson's Weekly*, and *Answers*. Others might be named, such as *Harmsworth's Penny Magazine*, but this triad are far in advance of all rivals; their leading position has often been assailed, but never seriously menaced. They constitute a suitable field for the early efforts of the aspirant, who should examine their pages with care. Broadly speaking, the popular weekly proceeds upon the principle that, although one half the world does not know how the other half lives, it would like to know. The popular weekly prints articles of which the titles begin with "How"—"How milk is adulterated," "How streets are washed," "How a public company is floated." Or it throws the light of its lantern on out-of-the-way occupations—"An Hour with a Horse-Dentist," "The Apprenticeship of a Steeple-jack." Or it collects together curious facts of a sort—"Crimes of Crossing-Sweepers," "Dogs who have brought Disaster," "Mill-girls who have become Marchionesses." Again, it prints mildly humorous sketches of social life, especially quarrels and reconciliations of married and betrothed persons. The aspirant may discover other features of the popular weekly for himself. He must not, if he happen to have a refined literary taste, despise the popular weekly. In nine cases out of ten, he may take it for granted that if he cannot please this class of paper he can please no other class. The popular weekly does not demand a high literary standard. And it pays very well—a guinea a column of five to seven hundred words, and sometimes two guineas.

It is most important that the aspirant should note the maximum length of the articles printed in every paper. The popular weekly, for instance, does not as a rule want anything over a thousand words in length. The first consideration with every editor is the length of the article submitted. If it is too long or too short, it may be the finest article in the world, but it will be refused. The aspirant should always count the number of words in his articles.

A secondary class of popular penny weeklies is now formed by *M. A. P.* and *T.P.'s Weekly*, both of which appeal to a slightly higher order of intelligence than the *Tit-Bits* class. *M. A. P.* desires personal paragraphs. And here I must quote from Mr. J. M. Barrie's novel of journalistic life, *When a Man's Single*, which every aspirant should read. A clever journalist in that book remarks to a beginner: "An editor tosses aside your column and a half about evolution, but is glad to have a paragraph saying that you saw Herbert Spencer the day before yesterday gazing solemnly for ten minutes in a milliner's window." *T.P.'s Weekly* has a literary cast. Both these papers offer opportunities to the enterprising tyro.

I come next to the daily papers. Of the penny morning papers the *Daily Chronicle* and the *Daily News* are the most hospitable to the freelance. The three principal half-penny papers, the *Daily Mail*, the *Daily Express*, and the *Morning Leader*, welcome outside contributions. Morning papers want short, very topical and timely articles or interviews, with or without illustrations. The half-penny papers have also a "magazine page," which is really a *Tit-Bits* day by day. The aspirant should try to get into this magazine page.

But the recognised lawful prey of the ambitious outside contributor is the penny evening paper, and especially the *Pall Mall Gazette*, *Westminster Gazette*, and *St. James's Gazette*. These three papers appeal to a literary public, and they demand from the freelance, whom they encourage, a high standard of style. Social sketches, interviews, and topical articles, will find a home in the "gazettes" when they are good enough. The other two penny evening papers, the *Globe* and the *Evening Standard*, each print every day an article, in the form of an essay not necessarily topical, which is frequently accepted from an outside source. This article is the first on the first page of the *Evening Standard*, and the last on the first page of the *Globe*. In both cases it is imperative that the article should conform to the requirement of length. The halfpenny evening papers will not be of much use to the freelance.

Next in order of importance to the freelance come the high-class sixpenny illustrated weeklies, the *Illustrated London News*, *Graphic*, *Sketch*, *Sphere*, *Tatler*, and *Black and White*. Of these the first and fourth are the most literary, and the second is the least benignant towards the freelance. All pay well, and one or two handsomely. And all are prepared to accept topical or personal articles, preferably illustrated by striking photographs.

The ladies' papers form an important class. The sixpenny organs are *The Queen*, *The Lady's Pictorial*, *The Gentlewoman*, and *The Lady's Field*. The first and last are best suited to the outside contributor; they pay well. The threepenny organs, *Hearth and Home* and *The Lady*, do not spontaneously encourage the freelance, but the latter buys occasional articles. The penny women's papers —*Home Notes*, *Home Chat*, *Woman*, &c.— appealing without exception to a popular public, do not offer much scope to the outsider.

The politico-literary weeklies should engage the attention of the serious ambitious beginner with a taste for letters, which, be it remembered, is not quite the same thing as a taste for journalism. The *Pilot*, *Spectator*, *Saturday Review*, and *Speaker* are open to receive topical and miscellaneous articles in essay form, with a literary or political turn. But they do not buy their views or their reviews from the outsider. The *Outlook* takes very short articles of a light texture. One or two of these organs do not err on the side of generosity in remuneration.

I cannot deal with the hundreds of weeklies which appeal to special publics, such as the *Athenæum* (literary), the *British Weekly* (religious), the *Investor's Review* (financial), the *British Architect* (professional), the *Draper's Record* (trade). The majority of them depend little on the outsider, but it is probable that very few of them would refuse to listen to an outsider who approached with an original idea specially suited to them. Some of them are very wealthy organs.

The monthly publications are divisible into three classes: general magazines appealing to a popular public; general magazines appealing to a cultured public; and reviews. The first class, of which the principal specimens are *Pearson's*, *Strand*, *Windsor*, *Lady's*, *Woman at Home*, *Lady's Realm* (6d.), *Royal* (4d.), *London* (3½d.), has the readiest welcome for novelty, and pays the best. Its articles are essentially *Tit-Bits* articles glorified in fine raiment; they must be illustrated. The second class comprises both illustrated—*Pall Mall Magazine*—and unillustrated—*Blackwood's*, *Cornhill*, *Longman's*, and *Macmillan's*. The unillustrated demand the higher literary standard. I shall discuss these magazines from the point of view of their requirements in fiction in a subsequent chapter. The "reviews" which pay for outside contributions are the *Fortnightly*, *Nineteenth Century*, *Contemporary*, *National*, and *New Liberal*. The aspirant need not trouble to woo these excessively *difficilé* old ladies until he has had considerable experience. A book dealing fully with magazine work is *How to Write for the Magazines*, published by Mr. Grant Richards, at 3s. 6d.

The foregoing conspectus of the British Press is, of course, far from complete, but it indicates the main outlines of the subject, and the aspirant must fill in minor details from his own observation and study. He must learn to differentiate the characteristics of one organ from the characteristics of another, and must thoroughly familiarise himself with the contents of every paper. He should on no account put any of the more popular papers aside as being beyond his enterprise. The less he limits the variety of his efforts, the more successful are his efforts likely to be.

First Efforts of the Freelance.

I have now shown how the third of my three maxims for the guidance of the freelance is to be carried into practice. I will go back to the other two. In choosing subjects to write about, the freelance must always bear in mind my first maxim. He may leave to great editors the task of educating the public; his own business is to minister to their desires. He must not be ashamed to be popular, and he must not be ashamed to write the kind of stuff that he would not dream of reading were it written by some one else. His first efforts cannot be too humble. The point is that he wants to get into print, and he will the most quickly and easily achieve his desire by appealing to a large audience. He must put away all sentimentality about the art of literature and the moral mission of journalism. It is of no use beginning to air one's views until one has collected an audience. A young man of talent, capable of distinguished work, may hammer at the doors of the *Spectator* and the *Fortnightly Review* for years with dissertations upon literature, morals, or world-politics; ultimately, when he has attained sufficient skill and shown sufficient pertinacity, he will be admitted within these august portals. I say that it would have been better for him, not only financially but in experience and in other ways, had he been content to make a start by amusing or instructing the populace. I would repeat and repeat again: Begin humbly.

It is well to begin with the paragraph. The piquant paragraph of two or three hundred words is enormously in demand. There is scarcely any paper with a general circulation that does not gladly buy paragraphs—paragraphs about anything and everything. Paragraphs are not a gold-mine, and only a freelance of miraculous ingenuity could make a living out of them; but they require much less constructive skill than even the shortest article, and just as completely as an article they afford the aspirant the satisfaction of seeing himself in print, and of pluming himself upon having established relations with a paper. The remuneration for paragraphs runs from half-a-crown to three and sixpence. Some papers pay by the inch, and some have a fixed price per paragraph irrespective of length.

My second maxim should help the aspirant in excogitating topics for his brilliant and facile pen. He must learn to see life interestingly. And he must fall into the habit of regarding the whole of human existence as material for "copy." The idea of "copy" must be always with him. When he jumps on an omnibus, ideas for articles should crowd thick upon him: "How an Omnibus is Built," for *Pearson's Magazine*; "The Ailments of Omnibus Horses: a Chat with a Vet. of the London General," for the *Westminster Gazette*; "An Omnibus Horse's views about Policemen," for a comic paper; "Ways of the Omnibus Thief," for

Tit-Bits; "London Stables: an Inquiry," for the *Daily News*; "Stopping and Starting," a sketch, for the *Queen* or the Saturday women's page of the *Daily Chronicle*. When he spends a sleepless night owing to the entire failure of all his efforts for a month past, he should by instinct consider the feasibility of a scare-article for the *Daily Mail* about the increasing use of narcotics by urban populations. When his uncle is killed in a great railway accident, he should be moved to write an illustrated article on the differences between ancient and modern railway accidents for the *Strand Magazine*. And when he is starving because he has been foolish enough to throw up a safe but modest clerkship before securing a position in Fleet Street, he should throw off a bright essay for the *Young Man* on "How to Live on a Shilling a Day." If he animates his existence by this spirit he is certain to succeed.

Matters of Practical Detail.

In writing a paragraph or article, always have in mind a particular paper, and aim at pleasing that paper. Do not make the produce first, and then try to select a market for it; but select the market, and make the produce definitely to suit the market.

Paragraphs and short articles need not be typewritten. Articles over two thousand words should, if possible, be typewritten. Without making a fetish of typewriting, one may say that it is never a disadvantage, and usually an advantage, to the journalist. And seeing that the best of all typewriting machines may be bought for half the cost of the best machines of ten years ago, the aspirant might well make an effort to possess a machine of his own. One shilling per thousand words is a fair price to pay for typewriting; in most cases to pay less is to countenance sweating.

When a contribution fills more than one sheet, fasten the sheets together at the top left-hand corner only with a paper fastener. Do not stitch or pin the sheets. It is well to protect the white sheets by putting a sheet of stout brown paper top and bottom. When these get ragged and soiled by postal journeys to numerous editorial offices, they can be changed. Never send out a soiled or torn manuscript; its condition always prejudices an editor against it.

Write on the first page of your manuscript the title of the article, your name and address, and the length of the article in words. Write your name and address also on the back of the manuscript.

Many papers print in every issue a few brief instructions to contributors. Read these before despatching your article, and make sure that you have complied with them.

Do not, save in special instances, send any letter with your manuscript.

Merely enclose a stamped, addressed envelope for its return in case of rejection. Note that some papers which state that they will not return rejected manuscripts, often do return them when a stamped, addressed envelope is enclosed. Always use envelopes, and not book-post wrappers, in order to minimise the wear and tear of your manuscript. If you wish to economise in postage (a serious item to the beginner), leave the envelope open and send it by book-post.

Take care that the envelope which you enclose for the return of the manuscript is large enough to hold the manuscript. Scores of beginners annoy editors by their carelessness in this obvious detail.

When a manuscript has been declined by a dozen editors, waste no further postage on it. Put it in a drawer marked "Frosts," and after a few weeks' interval examine it critically. You will then probably be able to discover why it failed to attract. I attach much importance to this examination of failures.

Remember that editors often make their preparations many weeks in advance. It is useless to send in Christmas stuff in the middle of December, or an Easter article at the end of March. The aspirant should buy or construct for himself a calendar of notable events, anniversaries, feasts, holidays, &c., and should keep well in advance of it.

When the aspirant has succeeded in contributing to several well-known papers, should have their names printed on his ca with the words "Contributor to." A card ornamented will often assist him to obt: both courtesy and information when in sea of material for articles.

Every serious freelance must have acc to a large public library, preferably the re: ing-room at the British Museum, which an inexhaustible mine of raw material for t journalist. The regulations for the issue tickets may be obtained from the Superint dent of the reading-room.

The difficulty of obtaining personal int views with editors or their responsible assi ants is greatly exaggerated in the popu mind. These sultans or viziers can usua be seen by the man who is calmly det mined to see them. But the aspirant sho not approach them unless he has a defin proposal to make, and until he can furn credentials as to his capacity.

All magazines, many weeklies, and a dailies send proofs of accepted articles correction. The correction of such proofs—which have already been corrected by a "reader"—is a quite simple affair, and need not frighten the veriest tyro. In the Appendix (pp. 226, 227) will be found a practical illustration and explanation of the principal signs used in proof-correcting.

In the matter of remuneration, one or two papers pay on acceptance, but they are seraphic exceptions. Some papers pay during the week following publication, and some during the month following publication. The accountants of some papers are not to be relied upon. Some papers, even wealthy papers, will never pay until they are asked, and even then as little as possible. Some papers, and among them several of considerable reputation, have invariably to be dunned before a cheque is forthcoming. If the contributor does not receive a cheque during the month following the month of publication, he should send in an account, giving the title, date, and length in inches of his contribution, and requesting a remittance.

Final Counsel to the Freelance.

I must warn the aspirant that he is bound to fail at first. Article after article will be rejected, and the process of rejection may continue uninterrupted for months. This is, indeed, the experience of ninety-nine out of every hundred beginners. But the aspirant should not be discouraged. He should persevere, and above all he should keep up a regular flow of articles. And while waiting for success he may positively assure himself that success does not tarry, (*a*) because his articles are not carefully read, (*b*) because the market is overcrowded with good stuff, or (*c*) because editors are fools. I need say no more in this connection.

Just as the aspirant is bound to fail at first, so he is bound to succeed in the end if he perseveres and directs his efforts with sagacity. Success, trifling to begin with, will increase; the standard of work will rise; and the time will certainly come when the freelance will cease to be solely a freelance. Either he will get a post on the staff of some paper with which he has gradually connected himself, or he will develop, as dozens of journalists do, into a novelist or some other kind of author. It is no part of this manual to deal with the duties of a staff appointment. I therefore pass to the subject of authorship proper, and in particular to the subject of fiction.

CHAPTER IV

SHORT STORIES

CHAPTER IV

SHORT STORIES

What Fiction is.

THE art of fiction is the art of telling a story. This statement is not so obvious and unnecessary as it may seem. Most beginners and many "practised hands" attend to all kinds of things before they attend to the story. With them the art of fiction is the art of describing character or landscape, of getting "atmosphere," and of being humorous, pathetic, flippant, or terrifying; while the story is a perfunctory excuse for these feats. They are so busy with the traditional paraphernalia of fiction, with the tricks of the craft, that what should be their principal business is reduced to a subsidiary task. They forget that "character," landscape, "atmosphere," humour, pathos, &c., are not ends in themselves, but only means towards an end.

The art of fiction is not the art of making an otherwise uninteresting story interesting by dint of literary skill and theatrical devices. It is the art of telling an intrinsically interesting story. The story itself—that is to say, the naked events or chain of events to be narrated—must be interesting. Imagine that you meet a friend after an absence during which something extraordinary has happened to you or to some one whom you know. You are brimming over with a choice bit of gossip. You cannot keep it to yourself. You break in: "Oh, I *must* tell you this!" And you begin. Perhaps the affair concerns people with whom your friend is unacquainted, and therefore certain explanations are necessary in order that he may grasp the full beauty of the situation. You are impatient because you cannot come to the point at once. "I must just explain first," you say, and you compress all preliminaries into the smallest possible space, but omitting nothing essential. And your friend says: "Yes"—"Yes"—"Yes," growing more and more interested.

His interest is kindled by yours. You never bother your head about atmosphere, landscape, character-drawing; yet all the time you are achieving these things unconsciously, in so far as they are necessary to the appreciation of your choice bit of gossip. At length you come to the central facts of the situation. You are preoccupied with *them*, not with the devices of narrative. The situation is so interesting that it wants no ornament, and what humour or pathos or wit comes out of it, emerges naturally and inevitably, because it must emerge. You arrive at the end. "Now *is*n't that interesting?" you ask your friend with confidence. "Rather!" he exclaims. And you breathe with relief.

Now that is precisely the spirit in which fiction should be written. The writer himself should be tremendously absorbed in the story; which is equivalent to saying that the naked events, the plot, should be interesting. Part of the secret of Balzac's unique power over the reader is the unique intensity of his own interest in the thing to be told. This singular interest gives animation to the extraordinarily long descriptions and explanations which Balzac constantly employed. You can almost hear him saying to you as he pants heavily through these preliminary pages: "Wait a minute, wait a minute. It's absolutely necessary that I should make this clear, otherwise you wouldn't quite grasp the point. . . . I'm coming to the story as fast as I can."

Plot, therefore, is the primary thing in fiction. Only a very clever craftsman can manipulate a feeble plot so as to make it even passably interesting. Whereas the clumsiest bungler in narration cannot altogether spoil a really sound plot. Hence the beginner has special need of a sound plot. Some years ago there was a movement against the supremacy of plot, or subject, in art. The cry was—"Subject is nothing; treatment is everything." The general public, following for once a classical ideal of taste, would not tolerate this theory, which has now died a natural death. I will quote from an illuminative essay of Matthew Arnold's, slightly altering the phraseology to suit the case. He says: " It is a pity that power should be wasted, and that *the novelist should be compelled to impart interest and force to his subject, instead of receiving them from it, and thereby doubling his impressiveness.*" I italicise this epigrammatic statement, because it is of paramount importance, and goes to the very root of fiction as of every other creative art. Matthew Arnold, who got his ideas from the Greeks, enumerated three principles as being vital to good art:—

(1) The all-importance of the choice of a subject.

(2) The necessity of accurate construction.

(3) The subordinate character of expression.

And the curious thing is that these three principles are vital not only to good art, but to commercial or popular art. It will be equally to your advantage to conform to them, whether your aim is to produce a rival to *Adam Bede* or to thrill the readers of a halfpenny paper with a sensational serial.

The very Short Story.

Much nonsense has been talked about the short story. It has been asserted that Englishmen cannot write artistic short stories, that the short story does not come naturally to the Anglo-Saxon. Whereas the truth is that nearly all the finest short-story writers in the world to-day are Englishmen, and some of the most wonderful short stories ever written have been written by Englishmen within the last twenty years. It has also been stated that the short-story form is exceedingly difficult, and that "the art of the short story" is an art by itself. This is not so. No one has yet shown wherein the art of the short story differs from the art of the novel. And there can be no doubt in the mind of any expert who has succeeded equally well in the short story and the novel that a short story is a simpler achievement than a novel. It may be easier to write a bad novel than a good short story, but it is manifestly absurd to argue that a good novel is easier to accomplish than a good short story. One might as usefully assert, in the art of music, that it was easier to compose a symphony than an "album-leaf," because in the symphony there was no restriction of space. Similar powers of observation, invention, imagination, and description are needed in the novel and in the short story. But the constructive power and the sustained strength required for a good novel far exceed those required for a good short story. The short story is the simplest form of fiction, and the shorter it is the simpler it is. The beginner should therefore begin with very short stories.

Process of Invention.

The minimum length of the short story of commerce is about one thousand five hundred words, and the tyro will do well to try that length. I will attend him in detail through his maiden enterprise. A work of fiction should properly take shape in the mind of the author in the following stages: —First, he should get a notion of the scene and general environment; then, the characters should present themselves, springing out of the environment; last of all, the plot should present itself, springing out of the characters. This natural order applies both to novels and to short stories; but it perhaps applies more particularly to novels; and in short stories the actual practice is often a reversal of the order. The central idea of the plot comes first, then the characters, then the environment.

The plot of a fifteen-hundred-word story cannot be much more than a mere episode. But, however slight a plot is, it must have a central idea; it must have a "point"; it must raise an issue and settle that issue; the interest of the reader having been excited must be fully satisfied. In other words, the plot must be complete; it cannot be a mere slice cut from something longer. In inventing his plot, the tyro should err on the side of melodrama and ingenuity, rather than on the side of quietude and simplicity. What he wants is a tale that "tells itself," a striking situation, a novel climax. Too much plot is better than not enough plot. I can offer no suggestions as to subject; the story may or may not relate to love; but it must not end unhappily—this is essential.

Having arrived at a fairly precise notion of his story, the tyro should write down the naked plot in two or three hundred words, or he should explain it to a friend. If the plot will not stand this test, it is not a good plot for his purposes. If it will, he may proceed, for a tale that looks interesting in outline will bear telling in full. When he has briefly sketched his plot in writing, and is convinced that it works up to a good climax and is complete in itself, he will decide definitely on the environment and on the minor details. The story ought now to lie before his mind's eye like a map. Small as it is, it will divide itself naturally into several parts. He must not begin the story with a piece of explanation. Begin always with action, so that the reader's interest may be aroused at once; necessary explanations and descriptions must come later.

Here let me insist on an extremely inportant rule of composition that specially applies to the very short story. Every part of a work of fiction should serve more than one purpose. If it is necessary, for instance, that a character should be described, the writer must not be content with describing it; he must devise such incidents as will illustrate the character in action. Assuming that for the proper effectiveness of his climax certain preliminary incidents are required, and also certain preliminary expositions of character, the writer might of course invent incidents which merely prepared the reader for the climax, and he might separately analyse and set forth the character; ultimately he would arrive at his climax. But how much neater, cleaner, more economical, and more effective, if he takes the trouble to invent incidents which serve the double purpose of leading up to the climax and of illustrating the character! The short-story writer, like the juggler who simultaneously spins a plate in one hand, tosses three balls in the other, and balances a stick on his nose, must know how to do several things at once.

The Execution.

Before he begins to write out the story in full, he must have a clear, accurate, and complete idea of what he is going to write; he must have meditated so long upon his subject that he is full and running over with it. He must have seen the scene, and he must know a great deal more about the scene than he can possibly put down. In order to increase the intensity of the imaginative effort which must accompany the writing of good fiction, he should take the story part by part and concentrate his mind entirely on each part as he executes it. In writing the opening bit of action, for example, he should think of nothing but that particular fragment. By this means, renewing the effort again and again as the story progresses, he will obtain better results than by dealing with the story as one indivisible whole.

He must be careful not to commit any *small* sins against the great law of Probability. In fiction, especially commercial fiction, you may steal a horse with impunity, but you are a rash fool if you look over a gate. In its essence, all fiction is wildly improbable, and its fundamental improbability is masked by an observance of probability in details. While the tyro, therefore, may be perfectly aware that his central idea is somewhat strained, he should tolerate no avoidable straining in the details of its execution. His characters may be compelled to act in a manner contrary to human nature, but they need not make speeches contrary to human nature. And even if they are compelled to make speeches contrary to human nature, they need not employ phrases and turns of speech which no living person ever did employ. For instance, when Dick Trevelyan, aged twenty-five, meets Lady Mildred Trefusis, aged forty, after an absence of seven years, it is extremely improbable that Dick would return thanks to Lady Mildred for having spoken nicely to him when he was eighteen; young men do not do these things. Hence Dick should not make any such speech to Lady Mildred. But if for the purposes of the story such a speech from Dick is necessary, even then he need not be forced to say: "It was extremely kind of you, Lady Mildred, to deign to take notice of an unlicked cub." Dick will more vitally impress himself on the reader if he talks as people do talk in real life. The writer must examine minutely every line of action and dialogue, and ask himself: "Now, is this right? Would this have occurred so? Would Dick have done this? Would Lady Mildred have said that in those words—?" And so on.

My tyro, before he has proceeded very far in his story, is fairly sure to get "stuck." There are two ways of being "stuck." Sometimes one *feels* what one wants to say, but cannot frame the idea in words, or cannot decide between several methods of presenting it. That way of being "stuck," is normal and healthy. Sooner or later the obstacle will disappear and progress will be resumed. But when the writer suddenly comes to the end of his ideas, when he begins to cast about idly for "something to say next," when he perceives an unbridged chasm between himself and the desired climax, then he should cry halt, and carefully consider his position, for he is on the way to certain failure. His best plan, under the sad circumstances, will be either to reconstruct the plot or abandon it entirely in favour of a new one.

He must arrive at his climax with verve and eagerness, or the story will drag. And when he has safely arrived at it, when the issue is decided and the reader's interest appeased, the tale must be stopped, ruthlessly, then and there. The end of the interest, of the curiosity, is the end of the story.

It is impossible to advise the beginner about the multitudinous trifles of fictional writing. But I shall make two negative suggestions. He should not, as most beginners do, make his characters either anarchists or literary aspirants. And he should not, as most beginners do, label his characters with old family surnames, such as Trevelyan, Trefusis, Anstruther, Lascelles, &c. And if possible he should find less hackneyed Christian names for his heroes and heroines than Dick, Gerald, Muriel, and Enid.

No rule can be laid down about writing and rewriting. Some men say best what they have to say once for all at the first writing. Others produce a very careful draft, and make only minor alterations in a final writing. Still others produce a hasty draft at top speed, and then rewrite entirely. The beginner, after a little experience, will discover his own method by instinct. The great thing is that he should not finish till he has done his best. Every man knows the feeling which follows a conscientious endeavour completely fulfilled. Every man knows whether or not he is justified in the boast: "I cannot make this any better than it is."

Models and Markets.

The aspirant should study good models. I am acquainted with none which will be more useful to him than the stories of Mr. H. G. Wells (*The Plattner Story*, &c., *The Stolen Bacillus*, &c., *Tales of Space and Time*), and of Mr. R. Murray Gilchrist (*A Peakland Faggot*, &c., *Nicholas and Mary*, *Natives of Milton*). The latter excels in the very short story, of two thousand words or less. But it will be useless for the aspirant to imitate either these authors, or any other first-class authors, in anything except their technique. I recommend them for their technique, which is unsurpassed. In the invention of subject the aspirant must, after he has carefully studied the market, be guided solely by his own idiosyncrasy.

There is a heavy and constant demand for very short stories—"storyettes" as they are termed in the strange *argot* of the literary bourse. I know that some large buyers experience a difficulty in satisfactorily filling their orders. The reason is that the writer who has achieved any sort of position does not care to expend an "idea" on a two-thousand-word story at so much per thousand words, when at a trifling increase of trouble he can manufacture it into a four-thousand-word story at the same rate per thousand. Very short stories do not "pay" the writer who is able to dispose of his work easily. Hence the "storyette" is the peculiar field of the beginner. The principal buyers of this article are the newspaper syndicates: Messrs. Tillotson & Sons,

Limited, Bolton, Lancashire; The National Press Agency, Limited, London; and The Northern Newspaper Syndicate, Kendal. Some halfpenny evening papers, one or two magazines, and very many weekly papers publish a "storyette" in every issue. *M. A. P.* and *T.P.'s Weekly* both publish short stories of a rather superior class. The remuneration for fifteen hundred or two thousand words varies from one to four guineas. *Lloyd's Newspaper*, for instance, pays four guineas, *T.P.'s Weekly* three guineas, and a certain evening sheet one guinea. The chief syndicates are not niggards.

The Magazine Short Story.

When the aspirant has accomplished a few very short stories with a certain amount of satisfaction and of profit to himself, he may attempt a more elaborate form. The average short story of the monthly magazines and the sixpenny weeklies varies from four to six thousand words; five thousand words is probably the mean—a length which gives ample scope for the display of literary ingenuities of all sorts. In the following magazines a melodramatic or strikingly humorous plot is essential, and the literary standard is a popular one: *Pearson's*, *Strand*, *Windsor*, *Royal*, *Harmsworth's*. The *Pall Mall Magazine* and the sixpenny weeklies print stories of all standards and kinds of plot. The readers of *Cornhill*, *Blackwood's*, *Longman's*, and *Macmillan's* are more refined and exacting in their tastes; while not objecting to a melodramatic plot, they like also stories of domestic quietude and social observation; and in any case they demand at least a colourable imitation of style. *Blackwood's*, in my opinion, still marks the summit of literary distinction, and the writer who is good enough for *Blackwood's* is destined for success. The other end of the scale, in a purely literary sense, is reached in some of the ladies' monthlies.

The aspirant will do well to aim at the most popular magazines. Though their editors are extremely exigent, their conditions are perhaps less difficult to satisfy than those laid down in magazines appealing to a smaller audience. Other things being equal, it is easier, I am convinced, to write a crudely effective, ingenious, "breezy" story of crime or mystery for the *Strand* than a quiet naturalistic study of social manners for *Cornhill.* In the popular magazines ingenuity of plot is almost everything, and a mere beginner may in a happy moment hit on a notion that will "sell itself."

The advice which I have already given as to writing very short stories applies to larger stories, and indeed to all fiction. In the very short story limitations of space compel even the beginner to confine himself strictly to the telling of the story. But with five thousand words at his disposal the beginner may fall into the common error of interrupting the action of his tale by passages which please him personally but which in reality are digressions. He should therefore examine his more elaborate work with a particular care. He should say to every paragraph, every incident: "Do you help the story along? Are you absolutely necessary to its progress and effectiveness? If not, out you go, no matter how fine you look!" He should beware of long explanatory passages. Should these seem to him dull and heavy, he must either forcibly enliven them by humour or other device, or he must cut them out and invent action to do their work. Every part of the story must be interesting, must titillate or give a fillip to the reader's curiosity and pleasure. Every sentence must inspire the reader with a wish to read the next sentence. This is "readableness," and the quality of "readableness" can only be obtained by constant effort, by a tireless intention to make the story "go" at any cost.

With regard to models for the five-thousand-word story, they exist in plenty. But some of the very best short-story writers make bad models, either because the beginner is likely to mistake their faults for their excellences, or because their methods and their effects are so peculiar to themselves, so individual and defiant of analysis, as to bewilder instead of assisting the student of them. Four of the finest living short-story writers are Mr. Joseph Conrad, Mr. W. W. Jacobs, Mr. Rudyard Kipling, and Mr. Eden Phillpotts. But I would bring forward none of them as models. On the other hand, "Q" (*Noughts and Crosses*, &c.), Mr. Arthur Morrison (*Tales of Mean Streets*), Mr. H. D. Lowry (*Wreckers and Methodists*), and Messrs. Wells and Gilchrist, whom I have previously recommended, ought to be of considerable use to the intelligent student. Of strictly popular writers, the cleverest and most workmanlike are Mr. Max Pemberton and Mr. E. Phillips Oppenheim. And if the aspirant is desirous of becoming a pillar of the popular magazines, he should ponder upon the works of these writers.

The demand for magazine stories is good, and of course it remains quite unaffected by the vicissitudes of trade, the rumours of war, and the preoccupation of politics. Last autumn I obtained some statistics from the editors of well-known magazines as to the number of short stories which they consumed in the course of a year. The figures were :—

Strand Magazine . . .	62
Pall Mall Magazine . . .	63
Pearson's Magazine . . .	67
Harper's Magazine . . .	88

The fiction-manager of Messrs. Tillotson's syndicate informed me that he bought annually about two hundred short stories of various lengths.

The remuneration offered by the principal magazines varies from good to generous. Periodicals such as *Pearson's*, *Strand*, and *Windsor* will pay as much as fifteen guineas to an unknown writer for a five-thousand-word story. *Cornhill* pays a guinea a page, which is slightly less. The *Pall Mall Magazine* does not care to pay more than two pounds a thousand. The threepenny magazines can be induced to give thirty shillings a thousand. The aspirant should walk warily into the webs of magazines which have outlived their reputations or have never acquired a reputation. I know of one magazine with an ancient name whose fixed price for short stories is half a guinea—not per thousand words, but per story.

CHAPTER V

SENSATIONAL AND OTHER SERIALS

CHAPTER V

SENSATIONAL AND OTHER SERIALS

The Serial Generally.

The serial story is becoming more and more a recognised feature of weekly and daily journalism. Even the weekly edition of *The Times* has its serial. Almost all the first class London weeklies, almost all the second class and inferior weeklies, almost all halfpenny dailies, London and provincial, and practically all provincial weekly papers, run serials. The magazines also run serials; but, in the matter of serials, the aspirant may ignore the magazines, and the more famous London weeklies too, as being beyond his reach. The lower class weeklies, however, and the London and provincial halfpenny dailies, and the provincial weeklies, should come within the purview of the ambitious aspirant. Quite recently I had cognisance of a case in which a beginner disposed of his first attempt at a serial to a London daily.

The majority of all serials, save those appearing in magazines and a few famous weeklies, pass through the hands of the three syndicates whose names I have given in the previous chapter. A director of one of these syndicates, a merchant who probably buys and sells more fiction than any other man in England, once told me that he divided serials into three classes—sensational, detective, and domestic; the second class is of course really a branch of the first; and he said that his favourite lengths were, for sensational serials twelve weekly instalments, for detective serials ten instalments, and for domestic serials fifteen instalments. The average length of an instalment is five thousand words.

Manufacturing a Sensational Serial.

Now we have here a forcible illustration of the general truth which I emphasised in

Chapter III.—that length is a primary consideration. The conditions of newspaper production make it imperative that certain features of an issue should occupy a certain space, no more and no less. And experience has proved that readers tire more quickly of an acute, thrilling interest than of a mild interest. Accordingly the number of divisions and of words in a serial has become fixed. The writer of a serial, therefore, if he wishes to succeed, must start out with the idea of a number of instalments, or compartments, of a given size. Since the syndicates are the chief buyers, he will do well to aim at the syndicates, who cater principally for provincial dailies and weeklies. Assuming that he proposes to undertake a sensational serial, he must always keep uppermost in his mind a plan-like arrangement of twelve compartments of five thousand words each. The central theme of his plot must be amplified in such a manner as to fill these compartments. The aim of a serial story is not merely to divert the reader line by line and chapter by chapter, but to induce him to buy the next number of the paper. Hence the good sensational serial has a "curtain," that is to say, an exciting, unsolved situation, at the end of every instalment. The good serial is a chain of episodes leading up to one grand climax—the determination of a destiny, the explanation of a mystery, or the detection of a crime; and it is also a series of groups of episodes, each closing with a partial climax.

The aspirant must never lose sight of this mechanical substructure, which is essential. A poor plot may prove saleable if it is handled in conformity with the rules; the best plot in the world will be fatally vitiated if the rules are transgressed.

Most serials, even the serials of "old hands," are manufactured in the wrong way. The writers begin their plots at the beginning instead of at the end. They invent the mystery first and the explanation second. I am convinced that this is wrong. Sensational serials are a comparatively easy branch of fiction (for which reason I treat them next after short stories), provided they are handled with common-sense. The device of the serial is to present to the reader a problem. The problem consists of a number of various circumstances, some of which contain the means of solving the problem and some of which do not. The latter circumstances are made prominent in the opening of the story, and the former are made prominent towards the close. Now it is surely obvious that the difficulties of contriving the plot will be simplified, and the effectiveness of the plot increased, if the writer has begun by deciding what the end of the tale is. It must be more difficult to invent a crime or other event which will exactly fit a previously-fixed set of episodes, than to begin with a crime or other event and then surround it with suitable episodes; just as it is easier to fit a stick accurately into a hole in the ground by making the hole *with* the stick, than by making the hole with your finger and then cutting the stick to match the hole.

Consequently, when the popular author,

asked by the ecstatic interviewer how he writes his wonderful stories, states, as he sometimes does, that he first gets his heroine into the most dreadful dilemma he can conceive and then proceeds to get her out again, he shows that he is a clumsy workman who has not properly mastered his craft.

Some Points.

In working out the details of the plot of a sensational serial, the beginner should attend to the following points :—

(1) There must be no preliminaries. The story itself must start at once, in the first few lines, and by the end of the first instalment not only must it be in full career, but all explanations must have been disposed of.

(2) It is unwise to have too many interests or too many characters. A main plot and a sub-plot will be sufficient. The more completely the main interest is centralised in one or two characters the better.

(3) On the other hand frequent and vividly contrasted changes of scene are advisable.

(4) The sensational serial makes no pretence of realism. Therefore avoid all truthful subtlety of characterisation and dialogue. Draw the characters broadly. Make the heroines beautiful, the heroes brave, the villains villainous, and the conversations terse and theatrical.

(5) Incident must be evenly and generously distributed.

(6) Avoid long paragraphs.

(7) Avoid scenes of squalor or poverty, except as an occasional foil to the atmosphere of wealth and splendour which should for the most part prevail.

(8) Rouse the reader's curiosity and leave it unsatisfied at the end of every instalment, except, of course, the last.

There is plenty of scope, even within these prescribed conditions, for the exercise of the inventive and constructive faculties, and of the imagination. I can find no reason why the sensational serial should not be deemed a legitimate form of literary art, and I would advise the cultured aspirant not to pour out his scorn upon it. As a training in plot construction and in narrative, the composition of sensational serials is decidedly valuable.[1]

Sensational serials sell at moderate prices. The syndicates will rise to thirty shillings per thousand when they are "well suited"; but a more ordinary rate of pay is a pound per thousand, and this, having regard to the fact that sensational stuff, after it is planned out, can be written very quickly, is not an inadequate return to an unknown author. It is quite possible for a sixty-thousand-word serial to be written in a month, and I have heard several serialists boast that they compose on the average five or six thousand words a day. A serialist with a reputation will naturally command higher wages than a serialist without a re-

[1] The beginner should study the works of Dumas the elder and of Eugène Sue. Also *More New Arabian Nights*, by R. L. Stevenson; *Armadale*, by Wilkie Collins; *Cold Steel*, by Mr. M. P. Shiel; *Dracula*, by Mr. Bram Stoker; *Monsieur Lecoq*, by Emile Gaboriau; and *The Murders in the Rue Morgue* and *The Purloined Letter*, by E. A. Poe. The most popular newspaper serialists of the day are Mr. Richard Marsh, Mrs. C. N. Williamson, Mr. W. Le Queux, and Miss Esther Miller.

putation, and his prices sometimes ascend to six pounds a thousand—seldom higher.

The aspirant should note that some of the largest newspaper firms keep a regular expert in serials, whose duty it is to discuss plots with the authors of plots, and to supply ideas, suggest improvements, and generally act as literary uncle to the author. This system is, in my opinion, of doubtful advantage to the newspapers, and it puts the author, who never knows when his work is done, indubitably at a disadvantage.

Domestic and Other Serials.

Not much needs to be said about domestic serials. The same general rules of composition apply to them as to sensational serials, though in a milder form. They must interest from instalment to instalment, but they must not excite. A large class of people positively resent being thrilled by a work of fiction, and the domestic serial is meant to appeal to this class. The theme must relate to love, and it must be treated sentimentally. The demand for purely domestic serials by unknown authors is not a brisk one.

Boys' serials form a separate minor branch of the craft. They may be divided into two classes—stories of school life and stories of adventure in foreign lands. They always ignore the subject of love. The principal boys' papers are *The Boys' Own Paper* and *The Captain.* Prices are not brilliant, and since the market is a limited one, it has a tendency to become the monopoly of a few writers. Similar remarks apply to serials for girls, except that the editors of periodicals for girls will not have really adventurous serials, despite the notorious fact that girls enjoy boys' books more than boys enjoy them. The one mistake of policy in that admirably conducted periodical, *The Girls' Own Paper*, has been that it never ran a serial by the late G. A. Henty.

There remains one other class of serial—the novel of the famous author which is published serially, not because it is specially suitable for a serial, but because it is not entirely unsuitable, and because the author's name will insure for it a favourable reception. When the aspirant has arrived at the state of being famous, he may compose without trammelling himself by instalments, regular partial climaxes, or fixed quantities of words. If his fame is sufficiently dazzling, and his work is fairly optimistic and cheerful, he will find that editors are prepared to waive in his favour even the sternest rules of serialisation.

Novelettes.

The novelette is the least glorious form of imaginative literature. It is issued in paper covers, usually at a penny, and may be said to be neither a serial nor a book. I have practised nearly every form of literary composition, but not the novelette, and my remarks on it are therefore not based on personal experience. I have, however, obtained information from professional novelettists.

The length of the novelette varies from

13,500 to 40,000 words; the average is 25,000 words. There are two varieties—the love tale and the religious love tale. The aspirant who wishes to make the experiment of writing a novelette should spend sixpence in a few samples. The principal publishers of them are Messrs. Harmsworth, Horner, Brett, Henderson, Shurey, and the Aldine Press of London, Buxton of Manchester ("The Halfpenny Novelette"), Heywood of Manchester, and Leng of Dundee ("Aunt Kate's Penny Novels"). The aspirant will perceive that these amiable inventions appeal to an extremely low but extremely virtuous order of intelligence, and that they consist of what the superior person would call sheer drivel. But what is one woman's drivel is another woman's George Eliot. All literary excellence is comparative.

The rate of remuneration for novelettes is not princely. It varies from two guineas to thirteen guineas for 25,000 words; that is, from one shilling and eight pence to about eleven shillings per thousand. The religious novelette commands the smallest price. As one novelettist epigrammatically put it to me: "The smaller the pay, the more of the Gospel."

These figures may startle the inexperienced. It must be admitted, however, that the amount of brains necessary to the manufacture of a novelette does not greatly surpass the amount of money paid for it. Those who are capable of more skilful work should attempt it, but there must be a number of women, perhaps clever women, who have a slight literary faculty and just enough brains to spare from other work to concoct a dozen or so novelettes per annum; such women may care to attempt the enterprise, and to accept the trifling reward.

I am assured that there is a large and steady demand for novelettes, and that a practised novelettist with a good connection may rely on continuous employment. Three thousand words of a novelette can be comfortably written in a working day of five hours, and the maximum income of the profession seems to be about three hundred a year.

CHAPTER VI

THE NOVEL

CHAPTER VI

THE NOVEL

The Sustained Effort.

It is much easier to begin a novel than to finish it. This statement applies to many enterprises, but to none with more force than to a long art-work such as a novel or a play. In the first place, a novel or a play should raise an interesting issue, and settle that issue in a convincing and satisfactory manner. And obviously the former part of the task presents fewer difficulties than the latter. Herein lies the reason why the last act of an average play is nearly always the worst, and why more people read the first chapter of a novel than read the last. In the second place, the sustained effort necessary for the composition of a novel or a play is really very considerable. Even the twenty thousand words of a four-act play cannot be decently achieved by an intelligence that has not been self-trained to stedfastness. And the eighty thousand words of a novel imply extraordinary dogged perseverance in an exhausting emotional endeavour. Instead of losing power as he proceeds, the novelist must be continually drawing on his reserves for additional power. He must "work himself up" at the start, and not once can he allow himself to descend from the lofty plane of emotional excitement on which alone creative work is properly accomplished. He cannot see all his work at once as the painter sees his canvas. Imagine the technical difficulties of a painter whose canvas was always being rolled off one stick on to another stick and who was compelled to do his picture inch by inch, seeing nothing but the particular inch which happened to be under his brush. That difficulty is only one of the difficulties of the novelist.

I mention these things in order to emphasise the formidableness of the novel. The beginner should not commence his first novel without the consciousness of a high resolution. He must dwell on the immensity of that which he has undertaken. He must gird his loins for the journey. He must eat the literary passover. He must take breath for the plunge. He should feel as a man feels who has determined to propose to a woman, or to give up smoking, or to save half his income. If he omits these preliminary mental formalities, if he forgets to furnish himself in advance with a great stock of resolution, perseverance, and energy, the chances are in favour of a fiasco, with consequent loss of self-respect and self-confidence.

It cannot be too fiercely insisted upon that a novel which is begun casually during a brief period of leisure and lightly taken up from time to time as occasion serves, will never be a good novel. While a novelist, especially a beginner, is writing a novel, the novel must be "on his mind," and it must be waiting for him at the back of his intelligence even when he is engaged on other things. It must keep him awake at nights, and wake him after he has gone to sleep. It must intrude itself on his attention, must be his hourly companion, like a profound grief or anxiety. I say "grief or anxiety" rather than joy. For it is a fact that few novelists enjoy the creative labour, though most enjoy thinking about the creative labour. Novelists enjoy writing novels no more than ploughmen enjoy following the plough. They regard the business as a "grind"; some of the most successful hate their profession; some of the greatest artists in fiction have never found themselves able to write except under absolute exterior compulsion. Whereas some of the least gifted novelists are known to find a mild pleasure in their work. Hence the beginner who begins with ardour and then discovers that the zest quickly fades, should not argue therefrom that he has no vocation; he should rather nerve himself and set his teeth and clench his hands for a continuance of effort. The mysterious impulse which drove him to begin is a better proof that he has the vocation than his disgust and repulsion in the midst of the task are a proof that he has it not. There are moments in the working-day of every novelist when he feels deeply that anything—road-mending, shopwalking, housebreaking—would be better than this eternal torture of the brain; but such moments pass.

The best proof of a vocation for the novel is that abstention from fictional composition should produce a feeling of uneasiness, dis-satisfaction, and guilt. A talent never persuades or encourages the owner of it; it drives him with a whip.

To Begin.

I will assume that the beginner has come to the tremendous decision of writing a novel —not a mere serial, not something that can be cut up into instalments, but a novel, a volume, an affair that will be printed on hundreds of pages, bound in cloth, sold at six shillings, and passed and repassed over the counters of Mudies' and Smiths'. And the beginner says, "How ought I to begin?" There are numerous slightly different ways of beginning, including several quite good ones. But I shall prescribe one definite course, since I am persuaded that the aspirant prefers a single *recipe* or course to a choice of them.

Nearly all that I have previously said concerning the composition of short stories and serials may be said of the composition of the novel; and, equally, much of what I shall say about the novel will apply to the short story and the serial.

Selection of subject, as the reader will remember, is the most important thing in writing fiction. Here I may remark that the beginner with a genuine vocation will probably decide to write a novel long before a theme occurs to him. It is the vague desire to write *a* story, not a particular desire to write a particular story, which characterises the genuine novelist. Many people who have hit on an "idea" are moved to write merely by their chance possession of that idea, and not at all by a fundamental instinct.

The beginner should proceed through the following stages :—

(1) He will invent and elaborate the plot. Now the action, as I have before explained, should spring out of the characters, and the characters should spring out of the general environment. Therefore the first dim indefinable efforts of the imagination will be concerned with the environment. By the environment I mean the place or places where the action is to pass, the general class and sort of people involved, and the broad effect of landscape and other surroundings. The mind must ponder on these things until they begin to take shape. Then follows the conjuring-up of one or two (probably not more than three at the outside) appropriate principal characters. And at length, when these have shown themselves, the nature of the action must be considered and evolved. Of course it may well happen that the first naked hint of the proposed book will be a hint of an action or a situation, or of a character, entirely separate from any notion of general environment. This is quite normal and correct, but the beginner must take care to carry that hint backward to a suitable

environment *first*, and not forward into a detailed action until the environment and characters are more or less defined. Having arrived at a broad notion of his scheme, the beginner should write it out with all the literary skill at his command, and submit it to a friend for perusal and criticism. Let there be no diffidence or false modesty in pursuing this very advisable course. The preliminary sketch will perhaps extend to two or three thousand words.

(2) The act of writing it will tend to make it clearer and to expose hidden weaknesses, and the next stage will be to cure the weaknesses, to bring the strong parts into relief, and to amplify throughout. The process of amplification will consist of inventing subsidiary characters, choosing precise environments for various leading episodes, settling the leading episodes, and devising minor episodes. By this time the principal characters and scenes should exist with some completeness in the mind. The whole book should now be planned out into chapters according to the

main divisions into which the action naturally falls. The beginner must concentrate his powers specially upon the closing scenes of the tale, the solution of problems, the final effects on character. He must permit himself no shirking; he must grapple firmly with the difficulties which are certain to arise, and not leave them till he has devised a satisfactory way out of each of them. Time and energy spent here are well spent. A day over the plot before the actual writing has begun may save ten days later on. In the result, the beginner must have a list of chapters with brief particulars of the episodes in each, showing where the various characters enter the story and disappear from it, where descriptions are to occur, and so on. This catalogue of the contents of chapters need have no literary finish whatever; but it should be clear and fairly full, especially towards and at the climax.

(3) He may now commence upon the actual writing of the book. Let him bear in mind that it is unwise to begin with descriptions or explanations. He should plunge into the

action, and at once present some of the principal characters dramatically, postponing explanatory matter until the reader's attention has been arrested. In regard to the writing, he must spare no pains on it; he must polish every detail, however minute, in succession, and leave nothing unfinished behind him. He will probably begin his task in a glow of enthusiasm, and he must proceed with it in a spirit of absolute thoroughness and warm ardour until this first glow begins to cool. He may feel a diminution of his own interest at the end of the first or second chapter; in any event the reaction is sure to occur fairly soon. When it does occur, let him stop. Even if he has only written four or five thousand words he will find that in writing them he has acquired a much firmer grasp of the characters and the action than he had before, and for the first time he will really perceive what the book is going to look like, and what its atmosphere will be. On the other hand, he will also perceive for the first time the true immensity of the whole task in front of him, and he will be appalled by it.

(4) Therefore I recommend that from this the first point of his discouragement, he should proceed with the book in a rough and hasty draft, leaving minor difficulties for future effort and seeking only to accomplish the whole story, somehow or other, and rather helter-skelter, as quickly as he can. Of such a draft he ought to be able to write at least five thousand words a day, finishing it in a fortnight or three weeks. The book now exists; it is clumsy, imperfect, "scamped," very weak in many places; but as an organic whole it emphatically exists; and by the standard of his first chapter the beginner can accurately estimate what he has done and what remains to do. Conceive the business of writing a novel as the carrying upstairs of a mass of human life from the ground-floor of the daily commonplace to the higher region of imaginative beauty. Well, the beginner has now lugged the vast mass halfway upstairs to an intermediate landing, and it cannot tumble back again; it is safe where it lies, and it may be carried up the remaining stairs in pieces, piece by piece, slowly, at leisure. Moreover,

something complete has been achieved, a definite position reached.

(5) The beginner may now congratulate himself on the fact that more than half his work is done. He will return to his first chapter. Perhaps he will leave it as it stands; more probably he will decide that by rewriting it he can improve it out of all knowledge. And so, chapter by chapter, deliberately, using time like a spendthrift, he will rewrite the entire book. The hasty draft, in addition to performing the functions of a draft, will serve to keep him in touch with the story as a whole, and by its bulk and completeness will afford him always an ocular proof of what he can do when he tries; such a proof is very sustaining in periods of depression and apparently hopeless difficulty. Let me add that, during the final writing, the beginner should frequently read and read again the finished portions, and also the remaining part of the draft.

I shall now deal with various details of composition.

Characterisation.

The tyro usually thinks that in fictional writing there is a special conscious business of "drawing the character." There is not. Characters can not be "drawn"; at any rate they cannot be "drawn" convincingly. They can only be shown in action. As long as the character performs no mental or physical act, the character will not live. You may assert that your hero is clever or brave till your nib is worn out, but you will not convince a single reader of the fact until you make your hero act in a clever or brave manner. Characterisation can be achieved solely through the creator's own clear vision of the character.

When you have got your character on the scene, you must force yourself to see and realise him as an actual person. It is your own vision of him that counts. Let me reiterate: It is your own vision of him that counts. If he is clear to you, his sayings and doings will, without conscious management on your part, combine together harmoniously to produce a clear vision in the mind of the reader.

If he is not clear to you, the effect on the reader will be correspondingly blurred. There is no other method of arriving at characterisation. Of course a certain amount of exterior description and of incidental explanation or exposition is necessary. But such passages must be regarded merely as an adventitious aid to characterisation; they are not the characterisation itself.

Descriptions of figures are often useful, but descriptions of facial detail are almost invariably quite futile. If your heroine is beautiful, say so as briefly as possible; the rendering of facial beauty is the province of the painter, not of the artist in words. Marked peculiarities of feature or gesture should be noted, but on no account should they be frequently insisted on, so as to "label" a character. The "labelling" dodge is a bad one. It gives no real individuality to the person "labelled," and affords no insight to the reader. You may say that your villain, John Smith, has a trick of exclaiming, "Well, really!" And you may compel him to exclaim, "Well, really!" each time he opens his mouth. But the device will do nothing whatever to assist the reader to realise what John Smith truly is. If you encounter in the street a man with one ear every day for a twelvemonth, you may know nothing about him at the end except the fact that he has one ear.

Characterisation, the feat of individualising the characters, is the inmost mystery of imaginative literary art. It is of the very essence of the novel. It never belongs to this passage or that. It is implicit in the whole. It is always being done, and is never finished till the last page is written.

Dialogue.

Beginners experience a difficulty in deciding when to use dialogue and when to use simple narration. Remember that the aim of the novelist is to tell a story, and to tell it with the greatest economy of means. If the facts to be related can be given more succinctly and forcibly in dialogue, then dialogue should be employed. Sometimes the novelist cannot come to a decision without experimenting in both methods. It is better to use too little dialogue than too much. At specially dramatic points a few lines of dialogue are sometimes of immense value. Beginners often fall into the error of starting a conversation between characters for a certain purpose, and then continuing it after the purpose is achieved, merely because in real life the conversation would not have ended when the purpose was achieved. This is bad art. The novelist's business is not at all to set down complete portions of real life, but only such fragments as suit his artistic ends. When a conversation has served its purpose, stop it instantly; if advisable you may summarise its conclusion in a few words of narration.

Dialogue in fiction cannot have the fulness of dialogue in life. That is to say, it cannot be entirely realistic. It must be rigorously selected. The novelist will not write down, therefore, what his characters, considered as actual people, probably would have said under the given circumstances. Having discovered for himself what they probably would have said, he will manipulate and compress it so as both to effect his artistic purpose and to deceive the reader into an illusion of reality. The illusion of reality will not be given unless the novelist, while departing from what the characters *would* have said, is careful to set down nothing but what they *could* have said. Thus, for a simple example, if he makes a peasant use a five-syllable verb, he may be as ingenious as he likes, but he will destroy the illusion of reality.

In the employment of dialect the novelist should never even approach realistic exactitude. The merest indication of dialectal peculiarity in a spoken sentence should content him. The speech of educated persons is full of small divergences from absolute correctness, but no novelist ever dreams of recording the hundredth part of such divergences. To do so would be to irritate and confuse the reader. In dealing with those more marked eccentricities of speech which constitute dialect, the novelist must exercise a similar discretion.

Landscape, &c.

No rules can be laid down in regard to the part which should be played in a novel by descriptions of landscape or other surroundings. Until the nineteenth century novels contained almost no descriptions of surroundings. At the present time it cannot be denied that they often contain vastly too much descriptive work. The beginner must act according to his own interest and his own vision. If his lovers are walking down a country lane, and it seems to him that the human figures are essentially part of the lane, and the lane interests him, then he must describe the lane by the light of his own sympathy with it. If his lovers are seated in a rose-shaded corner of a Belgravian drawing-room, and appear to him in unison with, and inseparable from, these surroundings of a luxurious and decadent civilisation, then he must describe the drawing-room; perhaps the pattern of the wall-paper or the curves of the coal-box may help him to define his characters. If, on the other hand, he is preoccupied only with his lovers, and sees nothing but them—sees them apart from the world, like figures against a background of brown paper—then he must not force himself to invent detailed environments merely because he has noticed that Mr. Henry James gives ten pages to the interior of a local post-office, or Mr. Eden Phillpotts four pages to a mountain stream. He must act fearlessly on his own initiative; no one can choose for him; he will be judged solely by the results he attains.

Episodes.

It may be said roughly that a novel is an organic succession of episodes, each of which has a little life and entity of its own. The beginner must severely interrogate each episode as he does it, and put it through a sort of cross-examination in order to justify its existence. An episode may be a beautiful and effective episode, but if it does not directly help forward the story as a whole, then it has no right to exist. Every episode must *directly* assist the progress of the tale. It is useless to urge that such and such an episode, though it does not help the actual story, illustrates a character or confirms an atmosphere. The subsidiary functions of an episode may be various, but whatever they are they must always combine harmoniously with the principal function of every episode, which is to *tell the tale.* When, for any reason whatever, you cease to tell the tale, you are sinning not only against policy, but against the classic principles of art. When an episode has been written, it is advisable to inquire: "Assuming that this episode were accidentally omitted, would the reader notice a hiatus? Would the actual tale be impaired?" If the answer is in the negative, then that episode must go.

The remark which I made on page 144 about the beginner's difficulty in stopping a conversation in mid-course when it ceases to be useful, applies with equal force to all episodes. Whenever any scene has served its purpose in the general scheme of the book, at whatever point it loses its appositeness and begins to be perfunctory, stop it. Stop it ruthlessly, and proceed with the tale at the next interesting point further on. Passages which do not interest the author are not likely to interest the reader, and a book gains enormously by the excision of everything that is not strictly relevant, indispensable, and of paramount interest. The beginner will be astonished at the amount of stuff which may be eliminated without in the least spoiling the story.

Some Minor Details.

Publishers and the public prefer long novels to short ones. It is curious that the most popular novels of the day—those of Miss Marie Corelli and Mr. Hall Caine—are also the longest novels of the day. From ninety to a hundred thousand words is a good length, but there is no objection to a hundred and twenty thousand or even more. Only reviewers have a prejudice against long novels. The beginner should fix for himself a minimum of seventy thousand words. I am bound to state, however, that modern authors, running counter to the wishes of the public, show a tendency to make their novels shorter and shorter. More than one novel of less than forty thousand words has been issued at six shillings.

When the novel is finished it should be read aloud in its entirety to, or by, some discerning and patient friend, and then revised once more. This operation is extremely important.

It is advisable to have the manuscript typewritten in duplicate, since it may experience many vicissitudes before it reaches a printer's; the cost of a second copy is half that of the first. All the sheets should be stitched together, not wired, in one batch, and enclosed in stout brown paper wrappers. I shall deal fully with the question of negotiating the sale of novels in the chapter entitled "The Business Side."

It is impossible to advise the beginner about the kind of novel which he should write. But he may be advised not to write either a historical novel or what was styled a few years ago a "sex-novel." The historical novel is an exhausted form of fictional art; no historical novel with a spark of genius has been published for years, and the market for historical novels is very flat. The truth is that the historic convention has become stereotyped and lifeless, and until some powerful talent takes it in hand and rejuvenates it, the beginner will do well to avoid it. The sex-novel still lives and cuts a figure in the world; some of the best and some of the most notorious books of the past decade have been sex-novels. For obvious reasons, however, this particular variety of emotional narrative demands a tact, a discretion, an equipoise, which it is extremely unlikely that any beginner will possess.

A domestic novel of modern life, having a simple, strong plot conscientiously worked out with as much vivacity, colour, and movement as the author can command, is at once best suited to the beginner's pen, and most likely to find a sympathetic audience.

The Artistic Novel.

Fine taste in fiction is almost as rare among novelists as among the general public. The average novelist is but little more pleased than the average reader with the supreme masterpieces of fiction. The average novelist is decidedly not very interested in the progress of his craft—in questions of technique or the achievements of other novelists. Occasionally, however, one encounters an aspirant who is genuinely enthusiastic for the art of the novel, who dreams of artistic perfection first and of popularity afterwards, and whose curiosity about technique is quenchless. To such a man, in search of ideals, I would say that he will find a refuge from the insularity of English fiction in Russian, French, and Italian fiction. The *literature* of the novel exists chiefly in France. The beginner with artistic aspirations should read the *Journal* of the brothers De Goncourt, Guy de Maupassant's essay on Flaubert, Tolstoi's essay on De Maupassant, and the critical work of Ste. Beuve, Anatole France, Jules Lemaitre, Paul Bourget, and the Comte de Voguë. In English he should read the letters of R. L. Stevenson, Professor Walter Raleigh's *The English*

Novel, Professor Saintsbury's essay on Balzac, and Mr. Edward Garnett's essays on various novels of Turgenev. He will find in these various works an attitude sharply different from the ordinary English attitude towards the technique, the scope, and the aims of the novel.

In selecting classical novels for study, the aspirant should bear in mind that the supremely artistic novels of the eighteenth century were English, while those of the nineteenth century were French. The beginner who wishes to learn how absolute realism may be combined with distinguished and beautiful art should read Richardson's *Clarissa*, the first and greatest of all realistic novels of any period or country. Scarcely any English nineteenth-century novelist after Scott has made a general impression throughout Europe; and it is difficult to assert, in the face of a practically united European opinion, that the insular idols of our Victorian era are quite first-rate. They are not. The quite first-rate novelists of the nineteenth century are

Balzac, Turgenev, Tolstoi, and Flaubert. Most of the works of this unrivalled quartet are translated into English, and the aspirant should study them, not only for their technique, which on the whole is unapproached, but for their fine seriousness and their emotional power. Flaubert's *Madame Bovary* has the reputation of being the most perfectly achieved novel ever written; but between *Madame Bovary*, Turgenev's *On the Eve*, Balzac's *Eugénie Grandet*, and Tolstoi's *Anna Karenina* it would be futile to discriminate.

The English standard of technique in fiction has decidedly improved of late years, largely owing to the example of Stevenson. At the present time we have at least half-a-dozen writers whose work would pass muster anywhere in Europe. I do not propose to name them. I will only remark that they are not among the notorieties of the hour.

CHAPTER VII

NON-FICTIONAL WRITING

CHAPTER VII

NON-FICTIONAL WRITING

Two Kinds of Authors.

Outside the department of fiction, there are two kinds of authors—those who want to write because they have something definite to say, and those who want something definite to say because they can write. Now to the historians, theologians, men of science, and philosophers who constitute the former class, it is obviously absurd to offer any advice that would come within the scope of a primer like the present volume. Of course these experts of erudition and science have to learn to write—and some of them would undoubtedly write better than they do if they had pursued a course of training such as I have indicated in Chapter II. But, having acquired the craft of writing, of expression, they have, in a literary sense, nothing else to learn. Their concern is not really with literature, but with some non-literary branch of knowledge or speculation of which literature happens to be the disseminating medium. To these writers, therefore, only Chapters II and VIII of my book can possibly appeal.

Nor can much specific technical advice be offered to the second kind of authors—those who want something definite to say because they can write. Fiction is a distinct craft, with a vast body of tradition behind it, and governed by a number of more or less precise canons. Accordingly a certain amount of instruction can be imparted to the aspiring novelist; whereas to the aspiring general writer little can be said that is not vague and ineffectual, for the reason that canons for his guidance do not exist and never can exist. I shall be content to discuss briefly the principal branches of non-fictional writing which are open to an author who has no definite "line," but who possesses a lucid and agreeable style and is anxious to turn it to account.

1. Memoirs.

I regard this as the branch of general writing which at once affords scope for the highest intelligence and yields the best monetary return. The British Museum and other great public libraries are full of what I may call "personal-historic" material which is capable of being worked up—that is to say, selected, co-ordinated, and modernised—for the delectation of twentieth-century readers. The business does not demand elaborate expert knowledge, but it demands an instinct for getting at facts, a sharp eye for the "human interest," a sense of dramatic effect, and a vivacious style. "Human interest" is always a sure card to play in the game with the Mudie-subscriber, and I do not know that any one need be so "superior" as to despise it. For example, a general writer who did in really good style a book under the title *Love Stories of Great Statesmen*, would certainly find a publisher for it, and would almost certainly find a monthly magazine to issue it serially—and this despite the fact that the subject is of the tritest. But it would be necessary to do the thing with picturesqueness and vivacity. There have recently been issued two volumes which are superlative examples of the "memoir" department of general writing. I refer to Mr. Austin Dobson's *Sidewalk Studies*, and "George Paston's" *Sidelights on the Georgian Period.* The prefix "side" in both titles well indicates the restrictions of this kind of work. Aspirants who have a tendency towards the historical, a predilection for delving into antique magazines, biographies, and diaries, should read these two admirable books and learn to what distinction the art of research and compilation can be carried. There is always a market for discreet gossip about historical persons, places, and things, or about classes or groups of persons—for "footnotes to history," to use Stevenson's phrase. Many books in this vein are published every year, but the raw material is as boundless as the market for the finished goods. Possible subjects crowd into the mind. The field will never be exhausted.

When the aspirant has devised a subject, he should plan the scheme of the book and, having written a specimen chapter, should submit it to a publisher, by whom he will be either encouraged or discouraged. If he can discover no publisher willing to regard his idea in a favourable light, he should abandon it and search for a better.

As I have stated in Chapter I, the "memoir" book is usually issued at a tolerably high price, and therefore on the royalty system it is more remunerative, in proportion to circulation, than a novel.

2. Popular Biographies.

Popular biographies, both of dead and of living persons, are a prominent feature of modern publishing. There are numerous "series" of biographies; some series are entrusted to writers specially equipped for their task, others might obviously have been written by any persons with a tolerable style and a ticket for the British Museum Reading-Room. The aspirant with a turn for biography should examine the publishers' lists. Most firms who issue series are prepared to consider suggestions for additions to those series. Nearly every dead celebrity has been dealt with, and most living ones. But the demand for new works is constant; the field may and must be tilled over and over again. At the present moment popular biographies of artists are in vogue. (See No. 6.)

3. Books about Towns and Districts.

Another fashion of the day is the illustrated monograph on a famous town or district. Messrs. Macmillan's "Highways and Byways" series, Messrs. Dent's two series of "Mediæval Towns," and Mr. Baring-Gould's topographical volumes offer striking examples. Very few of the books in this vein which have come under my notice can be considered really expert productions, and there is no reason why the ingenious aspirant with an idea and some tangible proof of his ability to write, should not add to the growing piles of historico-topographical gossip. A writer with a desire to travel might pass three months in Timbuctoo, and make something more than his expenses by a book called *Highways and Byways of Timbuctoo.* I do not mean this suggestion to be taken *au pied de la lettre.*

4. Adventurous Travel-Books.

In old days the book was a minor result of the adventurous journey. In the present age, however, the adventurous journey is frequently undertaken solely in order that a book may be written about it. A few years ago the travel-book was at the topmost height of a truly extraordinary vogue. But quite recently that vogue has to a large extent diminished, and travel-books are by no means what they were. Nevertheless they still loom large in the announcements of publishers. Dr. Johnson noted more than a century since that they were, as a class, very badly written, and the criticism still holds good. Not the peril of the adventure narrated, but the interest of the narration, is the principal factor in the success of a travel-book, and travellers for literary gain should meditate carefully upon this truth. As travel-books are usually issued at a fairly high price, a moderate royalty combined with a moderate sale results in a quite passable monetary return.

5. Books about Princes.

There is a steady demand for collections of anecdotic gossip about royalties and royal scions of all countries and nearly all ages. The material for such volumes is plentiful, and one or two astute writers have developed the gossip of thrones into a regular department of book-making. These books require the minimum of literary skill. As a rule they are extremely bad in their technical aspects. No doubt a good one—well written, discreet, and free from the more atrocious manifestations of flunkeyism—would achieve a very satisfactory reception. Many books about kings and queens begin their career by serialisation in a magazine.

6. Miscellaneous Monographs.

Enterprising publishers are always ready to consider original suggestions for books, no matter what the subject. Sports and pastimes, social topics, and national institutions, seem to be continually in season. The publishing world is waiting, for instance, for a really diverting anecdotic book on the newspaper press in the nineteenth century. Non-technical compilations about the motor-car will infallibly be needed in the immediate future. The inventive mind will easily devise many similar notions. It should be stated that the financial reward of most monographs, and of practically all books which are suggested by the publisher himself, or which form part of a series, is limited by the fact that the publisher prefers to pay down a lump sum for them. This rule applies particularly to Nos. 2, 3, and 6 of my divisions. The price of short popular biographies runs as low as £25.

7. Children's Books.

Children's books have lately shared the decline of travel-books. A few years ago they were a "craze," and every one was reading them, except children. They became tediously brilliant beyond the comprehension of the youthful mind. A reaction is now in progress. All children's books may be divided into three classes — imitations of *Alice in Wonderland*, pure fairy tales, and plain non-witty stories about children for children. The first class is at a heavy discount; the second is exceedingly difficult to write; the third offers the best opening. The average remuneration for children's books is not high; indeed it may without exaggeration be called very low. I know of one first-class firm of publishers which pays £25 for all rights in a 40,000 word book. Some firms are willing to pay a small royalty.

8. Essays.

There is almost no market whatever for essays, and books of essays seldom see the light. An aspirant who is obstinately determined to be an essayist should endeavour to place his productions serially in the sixpenny weeklies and the half-crown reviews. If they happen to be surpassingly good, a high-class firm with a taste for letters and philanthropy may conceivably be induced to publish them in book form at its own risk; but the possibility of the author receiving any appreciable sum thereby is remote to the last degree.

9. Verse.

Mediocre verse finds a home in the magazines, and clever verse in the "Occasional" columns of the *Pall Mall Gazette* and the *Westminster Gazette*. The two *Gazettes* pay, I believe, one guinea per piece. The magazines pay from one to two shillings a line, and sometimes more. Mediocre verse can only be published in volume form at the poet's expense, and even then only through a third-rate firm. Clever verse is issued, often at a trifling profit, by a few good firms who make a specialty of it. A not unusual practice is that the publisher should pay the poet an *honorarium* of ten guineas for a small volume. Verse of genuine indisputable high quality is so excessively rare that it is certain of recognition and of an adequate publication. If it is well advertised and paragraphed, the profits on it are comparatively large. Setting aside the abnormal rewards of a poet such as Tennyson, it may be said that quite a little band of minor poets have made a tolerably regular and not despicable income out of verse during the last decade. I have not much hesitation in asserting that no imaginative author is surer of a sympathetic reception than a really good poet at the present day.

There is a clear and concise chapter on English versification in Nichol's *English Composition* (see p. 44).

CHAPTER VIII

THE BUSINESS SIDE OF BOOKS

CHAPTER VIII

THE BUSINESS SIDE OF BOOKS

The Beginning of Business.

When the book is written the troubles of the author are nearly over, but the troubles of the merchant with a piece of merchandise to sell are about to begin. Let the aspirant recognise clearly that the remainder of his enterprise is not artistic but commercial. Let him grasp the fact that he is going forth to encounter men of business on their own ground, and that it therefore behoves him to act like a man of business and not like a man of genius.

He should see that the typewritten copy is accurate, and that the sheets are fastened together in such a manner as to be easily handled and read by a person sitting in an arm-chair. His name and address, the title and description of the manuscript, and the length of the manuscript in words, should all be prominent on the first leaf, and the bundle as a whole should look smart, fresh, and attractive.

In selecting publishers for experiment, the aspirant should begin with the best and work downwards in the scale of importance. The best publisher is usually the publisher who publishes the works of the best authors. But of course he must select a suitable publisher; he can acquire information as to the suitability of publishers by studying the advertisement columns of the *Athenæum*, the *Publishers' Circular*, or other literary papers. From the character of the lists of the various firms there displayed, he will be able to form an idea which firm is likely to suit him best. Having decided that point he should despatch his manuscript to the chosen firm with the briefest possible letter. Under ordinary circumstances this letter should contain nothing but the offer of the manuscript with a view to publication and a request for its return in case of refusal. Of course it may happen that some explanation of the manuscript is necessary; if so, the explanation should be quite short. All minor explanations, all suggestions about terms and so forth, should be left to a later stage of the negotiations. The beginner sometimes has a foolish trick of stating in full what terms he is prepared to accept from a publisher.

Publishers and their "Readers."

It is almost certain that the manuscript will be refused by the first publisher to whom it is submitted. The beginner must not be discouraged, but must send it on to another firm and continue to send it on to other and still other firms until either it is accepted or he has lost faith in it. There are about seventy reputable firms of general publishers, and the fact that a manuscript has been declined by ten out of this seventy is by no means an absolute proof, though it may justify a presumption, that the remaining sixty will also decline it. The beginner should despatch the manuscript as long as he believes in its worth.

Many manuscripts have been refused by all the best firms and then successfully issued by a second-rate firm. An element of chance or "flukiness" must of necessity enter into the question of the acceptance or rejection of any given manuscript by any given firm. Publishers are human, and their "readers," or literary advisers, are very human. I speak feelingly, for I have been a publisher's reader. Consider what happens to your manuscript when it enters the publisher's office. In the first place, it is a mere item in a crowd, for a firm will receive perhaps twenty unsolicited manuscripts a week; a clerk coldly enters particulars of it in a book, and it is shoved aside with other manuscripts to await the casual inspection of a partner or manager. In the second place, that partner or manager, being human, will probably allow the pile of manuscript to accumulate until it looks formidable. He will then approach his task with fear and dislike; he will perhaps unduly hurry through his task. It is wrong for him to do so; it is bad policy for him to do so; but he is human; he is not an unerring, unresting, unhasting machine of literary discrimination; perhaps he has bought a horse and wishes to get home early in order to try it. You may think that such trifles ought not to affect the chances of your manuscript with an eminent firm of publishers. They ought not, but they do. Well, the turn of your manuscript comes; the great man glances at it; he does not know your name, and since nineteen manuscripts out of twenty by unknown authors are worthless, he naturally begins with a melancholy apprehension that yours is worthless. He hopes there is something in it, but he is afraid there is nothing in it. The merest detail may fatally influence him in those crucial moments. Remember that the great man is not reading your work; he is only tasting it to decide whether it is good enough to send to his reader. A single dull page, a sentence, a phrase, an unconscious irritation of one of his thousand susceptibilities, *may* ultimately cause him to cast your manuscript on the left, among the goats.

But I will suppose that he is vaguely impressed by your manuscript, and that he sends it to Mr. So-and-So for a detailed opinion. Now Mr. So-and-So has also been born in sin. He is a creature of highly educated taste, of honourable impulses; but he is mortal. He is either paid by a fixed salary or by a fee per manuscript; and in either case he wants to spend as little time on your work as is consistent with his duty. Reading books in typescript is not an agreeable occupation, and the fact that Mr. So-and-So passes many hours per week in that occupation does not make it the less disagreeable to him. In a word, Mr. So-and-So is rather bored by the prospect of reading your book. By a piece of thoughtlessness you may put him in a bad humour at the very start. As he settles into an easy chair, and glances at the clock, and faces the task, the walls of his study may hear him exclaim: "I wish these confounded amateurs would employ decent typewriters!" or "Why can't they pin their sheets together decently?" or "Spilt infinitives all over the place!" or "Fancy beginning right off with a thundering coincidence!"

Even if the reader gets interested in your stuff and actually thinks that it is good, he may decide against it on the ground that it will not be popular. Publishing firms flourish by making profits; and profits are made out of books that sell; and it is the business of the reader to recommend not good books merely, but good books that will sell. When a reader recommends his firm to publish a book, and the publication results in a loss of fifty pounds, the reader loses fifty pounds' worth of reputation; and if this unsatisfactory phenomenon occurs once too often, he loses the whole of his reputation and his situation also. Therefore, when he likes a manuscript but fears for its popularity, he thinks first of his reputation and his situation. Being a child of Adam, he prefers to run the risk of refusing a good book than to run the risk of compromising his reputation and exposing his employers to monetary loss.

The vast majority of readers' reports are

either unfavourable, or favourable in a half-hearted, cautious way. Not once in a hundred times does a reader recommend a book with enthusiasm. Readers, when they like a book, are disposed to say, in effect: "This book isn't half bad. On the other hand it isn't brilliant. The author may do better. On the other hand he may not. It doesn't really matter much whether you publish the thing or not. I won't prophesy a good sale, but on the whole I should be disposed to say that you would not be ill-advised in publishing it."

I will suppose that the reader has sent in such a report about your work. The report will probably annoy the publisher, who will remark satirically: "I wish these alleged experts of ours would make up their minds one way or the other! What do we pay them for?" If his lists are fairly full, he may unceremoniously decide against the book, despite the reader's mild approval of it. But vacancies in his list, or some attractive phrase in the reader's report, may induce him either to read the book himself or to submit it to another reader. In which case the martyrised manuscript has to undergo still another and perhaps more fearful ordeal.

Here I will quote from a letter written by one of the foremost publishers in London:—

> "I generally take very great care over the reading of books, first looking at the MSS. myself, and then sending those that seem worthy of it to a very good reader. There remains a further ordeal in the shape of a second reader, who is also first-class, and the unfortunate MS. has sometimes to run the gauntlet of a third reader. It does not follow that because a book is declined, the refusal is on the score of literary merit or demerit. Readers are human, and they have their fads and follies. It must sometimes happen that a MS., though containing real merit, offends the idiosyncrasy of the critic, who incontinently damns it."

These sentences sum up the matter with fairness.

I have given considerable space to the probable adventures of a manuscript in a publisher's office, because it is extremely important that the timid beginner should realise with precision the nature of those adventures, so that he may avoid the indiscretion of being either vexed or discouraged when a manuscript of which he thinks well is refused over and over again.

A publisher should not be allowed to take more than a month in deciding about a submitted manuscript. At the expiration of that period, he should be firmly and persistently dunned for either the manuscript or an acceptance. Years may elapse before a good manuscript finds acceptance. The beginner is inclined to say to himself that he will not commence a second book until he knows definitely the fate of the first one. This is a mistake. As an artist he should forget that the first one exists, and should enter upon a new enterprise immediately he has recovered from the slackness and depression which will be the natural reaction from the strain of completing the first.

A list of publishers, with their addresses and some more or less useful notes about their specialties and peculiarities, is included in *The Literary Year-Book*, published by Mr. George Allen.

The Agreement.

A publisher having at length expressed his willingness to publish the aspirant's book, if terms can be arranged, the next step is to settle the details of the agreement.

Now in certain circles of authorship a tremendous outcry has been raised that publishers are grinders of the faces of the poor, and common sharpers. That some publishers are dishonest tricksters is indubitable. So are some grocers, some engineers, some parsons, and some authors. Publishers as a commercial class are neither more nor less honourable than any other commercial class, and authors are neither more nor less honourable than publishers. In the world of commerce one fights for one's own hand and keeps within the law: the code is universally understood, and the man who thinks it ought to be altered because *he* happens to be inexperienced, is a fool.

The publisher has two advantages over the literary aspirant. First, he knows his business, while the aspirant doesn't; and second, the aspirant is usually more anxious to get his book published than the publisher is to publish it. The publisher would be a philanthropist and not a business man if he magnanimously refrained from using these advantages. To publish a book by a new author is admittedly a risky enterprise, and if the publisher exaggerates the risk, as he almost certainly will, the aspirant must comfort himself with the thought that at any rate the book is going to be published. To get his first book on the market through the medium of a high-class firm is after all the principal thing for the aspirant; the amount of profit to the aspirant is quite secondary. If he is wise the aspirant will regard his first book as an advertisement, not as a source of revenue. Publication of a first book through a high-class firm on less advantageous terms is better than publication through a second-rate firm on more advantageous terms. Let the aspirant note that of a book by a new author a high-class firm will sell more copies, and will command more careful reviews, than a second-rate firm. Reviewers are decidedly influenced, whether consciously or unconsciously, by the renown and authority of the name at the foot of the title-page of a book by an unknown writer.

Hence the aspirant who is negotiating terms for the publication of his first book must be yielding in a degree commensurate with the standing of the firm, and with the number of refusals which the manuscript has previously experienced. But as a rule—to which, however, there are a few striking exceptions—the greater the firm the more generous their treatment of beginners.

Many firms have a printed form of agreement, which they fill up and send to the author for signature. Sometimes this agreement is fair, sometimes iniquitous. It will be sufficient if the aspirant notes the following points :—

(1) He should never under any circumstances, if he means seriously to adopt the profession of authorship, agree to bear the whole or part of the expenses of publication. The entire cost of publication, advertising, &c., must be borne by the publisher.

(2) He should never, if he can possibly avoid it, agree to be remunerated on the half-profit system. The system is thoroughly bad. A thoroughly bad system may happen to work smoothly in rare instances.

(3) He may properly be remunerated in one of three ways. (*a*) The publisher may buy the entire copyright of the book outright for a lump sum down. (*b*) The publisher may buy the copyright for a term of years, say five or seven, at the expiry of which the copyright reverts to the author. (*c*) The publisher may acquire the right to publish during the whole term of copyright, or for a shorter term, by agreeing to pay the author a royalty on every copy of the book sold. In the case of a new author, who wants advertisement first of all, both (*a*) and (*b*) have advantages, since they obviously offer the publisher a special inducement to push the book. Of course (*b*) is better than (*a*). For a first novel £75 is a handsome, and £50 a fair, price for the entire copyright. The copyright for a term of years is worth very little less. On the (*c*) system, 10 per

cent. (7d. per copy) is a fair royalty on a first novel; a royalty of a shilling per copy is handsome. A well-established popular author can get 25 per cent. (1s. 6d. per copy), and one hears of 33 per cent. The aspirant who is to be paid on the (*c*) system should endeavour to arrange for a "payment in advance of royalties" on publication (say £20), but he cannot *insist* on this until he has made some sort of reputation. In systems (*a*) and (*b*) the price should be payable in full on the day of publication. In the (*c*) system accounts should be rendered and royalties paid half-yearly. There is no adequate method of checking publishers' accounts. The aspirant must trust to their correctness.

(4) The agreement should name a definite date on or before which the publisher is bound to publish the book. It should state the price of the book. It should also provide that the author receives six free copies, with the right to buy more copies at trade price.

(5) Some publishers insist on a clause in which the author indemnifies them against

the consequences of any action for libel which may be brought against them in respect of the contents of the book. In principle this seems to me to be a just clause, but the author should examine the wording of it. One well-known publisher reserves the right to settle or to contest any libel action entirely at his own discretion, but entirely at the author's expense. This is manifestly wicked. Some publishers make no reference to a libel clause.

(6) The aspirant should not trouble much about American copyright. It is exceedingly difficult to obtain American copyright of a first book. But if by happy chance it can be obtained, so much the better.

(7) Some publishers will offer to publish a first book on the condition that they have the refusal of the second book on the same terms. Such a condition is not to be recommended, but there are occasions when the author may be wise in submitting to it. He should, however, on no account tie up more than one book in this manner.

(8) The aspirant cannot interfere in matters which relate to printing, paper, binding, advertisement, and review copies. These important details must be left to the sole discretion of the publisher. But the aspirant may offer suggestions.

(9) The agreement will be executed in duplicate. The copy signed by the publisher will be handed to the author, and *vice versa.* Immediately on receipt of it the author should take his copy to a post office and get it duly stamped. Without a stamp it is useless. An agreement liable to sixpence stamp duty must be stamped within fourteen days of execution. If the duty exceeds sixpence the period is extended to thirty days.

There are innumerable other points concerning agreements which might be discussed; but I have dealt with all the points which are really important to the author of a first book. The aspirant with a legal turn who wishes for further information should join the Authors' Society (39 Old Queen Street, Storey's Gate, S.W.), which publishes a highly interesting and intricate literature on the relations between writers and publishers, and all the dreadful possibilities thereof.

Subsequent Proceedings.

After the agreement is signed, the author should get back his typescript and scrupulously revise and correct it, in order to avoid alterations and corrections (for which he may be called upon to pay) in proof. When the time for "setting up" comes, he will receive proofs from either the publishers or the printers. These proofs may be either in long "slips" or in page form, according to arrangement. They will have been carefully corrected before they reach the author, whose work on them (provided he has properly revised the typescript) will therefore be light. They will probably arrive in small daily batches, and they should be returned with promptness. If the corrections or alterations are unfortunately heavy, a second proof may be advisable. When he has finally passed the proofs "for press," the author will see nothing more of his precious and epoch-making book until the parcel of six free copies arrives on the day of publication. He should subscribe to a good press-cutting agency for cuttings of reviews. A novel or other book of a popular description issued by a good firm will usually receive upwards of forty reviews.

He should watch the advertisements of his book. An occasional diplomatic letter to the publishers in reference to advertisements may sometimes do good. An enterprising firm will advertise a book, especially a novel, four or five days a week in daily and weekly papers, for two and even three months. I have estimated, from my own personal observation, that certain publishers have advertised certain quite ordinary books between a hundred and fifty and two hundred times within the space of three months.

If a first book achieves a sale of a thousand copies it does very well. The average circulation of first books is probably nearer five hundred.

A Reputation.

It is best that a reputation should be made slowly. The greatest and firmest of modern reputations have been made slowly. When the author has produced something which the public appreciates, he should offer the public something else of the same sort, but better, as soon as possible. He need not be afraid of tiring the public by too much work; he will only tire them by perfunctory and hasty work. Critics are fond of crying out against over-production. One sees the phrase in the newspapers: "Mr. Blank is one of the few authors who do not over-write themselves." The truth is that only a small minority of authors over-write themselves. Most of the good and the tolerable ones do not write enough. They are in receipt of comfortable incomes and they develop a tendency to be lazy. This I know by auricular confessions. If the good and the tolerable authors wrote more, there would be less room for the perfunctory and the impudently careless authors.

The aspirant who has been fortunate enough to make even the smallest success cannot follow it up too industriously and pertinaciously. He should take care to produce books at short regular intervals. He may continue this process for years without any really striking result either in fame or money, and he may pessimistically imagine that his prolonged labours are fruitless. And then newspapers will begin to refer to him as a known author, as an author the mention of whose name is sufficient to recall his productions, and he will discover that all the while the building of his reputation has been going on like the building of a coral reef. Even mediocre talent, when combined with fixity of purpose and regular industry, will infallibly result in a gratifying success. But it must never be forgotten that while the reputation is being formed, the excellent and amiable public needs continuous diplomatic treatment. The excellent and amiable public must not be permitted to ignore the existence of the rising author. At least once a year, and oftener if possible, a good, solid, well-made book should be flung into the libraries.

When the reputation is fully achieved, and the author's talent arrived at maturity, then, and not before, he may begin to enlarge his borders and indulge his idiosyncrasies with more freedom. In other words, the compromise between his own taste and the taste of the public, to which every author except the greatest must submit and ought to submit, may be to a certain extent abandoned. It is difficult to make a reputation, but it is even more difficult seriously to mar a reputation once properly made—so faithful is the public. From an established favourite the public will stand even hasty work and insolence. Much more, therefore, will it stand original and novel work that is sincerely done.

Of course every author rightly wishes to make a position for himself as quickly as he can. And the author who achieves an early sudden success is to be congratulated—if his moral qualities are such that he can live up to that success. But an early success is a snare. The inexperienced author takes too much for granted. Conceit overcomes him. He regards himself with an undue seriousness. He thinks that he is founded in granite for ever. He thinks that the public will enjoy whatever he does because he has done it. Also he is tempted to expend his spirit prodigally in the service of editors and publishers for immediate profit, instead of working in secret for future and larger profit. The way not to consolidate a reputation is to fritter away energy on a multitude of small journalistic items instead of concentrating it on a single momentous enterprise. The young man with a small success to his credit may hug himself on the fact that he has got contracts for a regular weekly signed article in a sixpenny paper, a sensational serial in a daily, a hundred pounds' worth of short stories in various Christmas numbers, and so on. But it were perhaps better for him, artistically and financially, that he should have earned less current money and given more time to a large work. Literary reputations are made by books (the longer the better!), not by contributions to the journalism of the day.

All the foregoing remarks are addressed to those of my readers who do not happen to have very exceptional talent; that is, to about 99 per cent. of my readers. The man of very exceptional talent and the man of genius make rules to suit themselves, and break the old rules with astonishing felicity.

The Literary Agent.

The beginner, at the very outset, will do better for himself than any literary agent can do for him. A good agent with a busy practice will not, and cannot, devote to the work of a beginner, who *may* prove in the end profitless, that careful and minute attention which is necessary to ensure success. The best agents naturally decline to act for quite unknown men except on payment of a preliminary fee; and the preliminary-fee system is bad for all parties. When the aspirant has made a little success, when he can sell his work himself, then is the time for him to go to an agent. This advice may seem paradoxical, but it is sound. The value of a good literary agent to a rising or risen author has been demonstrated beyond all argument. The question of the literary agent is no longer a "vexed question"; it is settled. An occasional protest against the agent, as an institution, is raised in some organs of the press, but all authors familiar with the inside of Fleet street are perfectly acquainted with the origin of such protests, and they smile among themselves. The editor and the publisher who "cannot understand why authors should be so foolish as to pay 10 per cent. of their earnings to an agent," are marked men in genuine literary circles. When an editor or publisher informs you with a serious face that he never deals with literary agents, keep your wits about you, for you will need them. As a matter of strict fact I do not believe that there is a single editor or publisher of the slightest importance in London who could afford to boycott literary agents, for the simple reason that the work of nearly all the best authors can be obtained only through their agents.

An inefficient literary agent is worse than none. The number of efficient agents is exceedingly small. My personal opinion is that there are certainly not more than three. The young author should remember this, and not be led away by specious circulars. In no case should he pay a preliminary fee. If a good agent will not act for him without a preliminary fee, the aspirant may rest assured that his case is not ripe for agency. The remuneration of agents, 10 per cent. on gross receipts, may at first sight appear large, but actually it is not excessive, especially on small incomes. When an author's income reaches two thousand a year, the agent should be willing to accept 5 per cent. on all sums exceeding two thousand; but these details are not for the aspirant.

The agent cannot perform miracles. He cannot force editors and publishers to buy work which they do not want, or to pay more than they feel inclined to pay for work which they do want. What he can do is to suit the goods to the market and the market to the goods, to prevent the author from making an arrant fool of himself, and generally to exercise in delicate negotiations that diplomatic firmness and that diplomatic elasticity which are his chief stock-in-trade. The author who sells his own work when he might employ an agent to do so, commits three indiscretions at once. He loads his mind with preoccupations which impede the processes of literary composition. He meddles, of course clumsily, in a department of activity in which he is not an expert, and for which he is not fitted. And he loses money. It is almost universally true that an agent will get higher, and much higher, prices for a rising author than the author can get for himself. I do not think I am exaggerating if I say that when the average rising author goes to an agent, his income is doubled within twelve months.

An author should visit his agent frequently,

and keep him fully acquainted with his projects and plans. He should listen to the agent's advice, but should not follow it too slavishly. No man, except a greater author, can teach an author his business. The agent is seldom or never a real expert of the literary art. He is half an expert of the literary art and half a commercial expert: that is his *raison d'être*. An agent who was a real expert of the literary art would decidedly be a very bad agent.

Lastly, when an agent is negotiating the sale of a work, he has the right to expect that his client will not interfere in the negotiations in any manner whatsoever. On the purely business side, after minimum prices have been settled between author and agent, the author should trust to the agent implicitly.

CHAPTER IX

THE OCCASIONAL AUTHOR

CHAPTER IX

THE OCCASIONAL AUTHOR

Books by Non-Literary Experts.

In these days a man who has no general desire to write, and no sympathy with literature, may be led by circumstances temporarily to join the ranks of the authors. The inducing circumstances are entirely unconnected with the literary instinct; they have to do with the love of gain, the passion for notoriety, or—more seldom—the genuine wish to impart knowledge. Any man, for example, who happens to win the professional or amateur golf championship for three years in succession could certainly get a good offer from a good firm of publishers for a book on golf. He may be almost wholly unfitted for the task of writing a book; he may loathe the sight of a pen, the composition of even familiar letters may be a weariness to him; nevertheless a book by him on his subject will sell. The same thing may be said of the man who swims the channel, the man who spends twenty years in prison, the man who loops the loop, the man who squanders a million in three years, the man who gets in and out of Lhassa safely, the man who goes round the world in sixty days, the man who has achieved fame by devoting a lifetime to chrysanthemums, or bulldogs, or dynamos, or consumption, or the North Pole, or hunting, or old furniture, or safe-robbing. Sooner or later the idea will occur, or will be presented, to every conspicuous specialist: "Why not write a book about your speciality?" From such a volume the profits may be anything from fifty pounds to fifty thousand pounds. The literary sequel of Nansen's approximation to the North Pole no doubt resulted in the accruing of considerably more than fifty thousand pounds to the explorer's pocket, while even the Jubilee Plunger was able to make an appreciable sum out of the record of his jejune follies. Examples might be multiplied infinitely, and it cannot be questioned that the class of books by non-literary experts grows more numerous year by year.

The Amateur's Best Way.

When the non-literary expert is wooed by a firm of publishers, or himself conceives the idea of a book, he is often at a loss how to proceed. He cares nothing and knows nothing about literature, but he wishes to produce just that book, as well as he can, and with the least possible worry and trouble. To begin with, if the affair is sufficiently important—that is to say, if he is likely to make a hundred pounds or more out of it—he should put the business side of it unreservedly into the hands of a good literary agent. And he should also consult the agent as to the literary side.

Some non-literary experts have a natural gift of literary expression; every man who thinks clearly can write clearly, if not with grace and technical correctness. Most non-literary experts, however, write very badly—and who shall blame them, since neither thinking nor writing is their special business? The man who cannot write decently, and feels that he cannot, yet is determined to compass a book, should proceed as follows :—

He should forget that such things as style, literature, and print exist; and he should endeavour to convince himself that writing a book is exactly on all-fours with telling a friend about one's exploits, or writing a letter to one's mother to say that one has been made a K.C.B. or a 'Varsity Blue. (It is, really.) He should then plan out the various divisions of the subject itself, omitting all side-issues, digressions, prefaces, introductions, or other extraneous matter. He may next make short notes of the contents of each division. Then, taking the first division, he should thoroughly think it out in his mind, and when he is saturated with it, he should explain it all orally to a friend—any friend who happens to be handy. He will find that this process, if faithfully executed, will clarify and arrange his ideas in an extraordinary way. The time has now come for him to write out the first division. Let him write naturally, utterly forgetting style, spelling, punctuation, and everything that he has hitherto connected with the notion of literature. When he sticks fast over the expression of a thought, he must imagine the friend in front of him and himself explaining that thought by word of mouth, and he must write as he would speak. Above all, he must make no attempt to imitate professional authors by the aid of his recollections of newspapers and books. At all cost of dignity, sonority, and convention, he must be simple and unaffected. Doubtless he will think ruefully that this haphazard, schoolboyish, unconventional production which he is accomplishing is not in the least literature. He may be satisfied, nevertheless, that it is a nearer approach to literature than he could arrive at by any other procedure.

The Literary Assistant.

When he has finished the first division he may call it a chapter and regard it as part of a book. He should take it to his agent, if he has employed one, and ascertain whether it will "do." He may rely on the agent's candid opinion. If he has not employed an agent, he must get the best opinion available. Should the opinion be favourable, the amateur author may of course continue as before. Should the opinion be wholly or mainly adverse, he must call in a literary specialist to his assistance. He may be introduced to such a person by his agent, or the editor of any literary paper would be happy to make a recommendation. This literary assistant is an inexpensive luxury and well worth his cost. He will either work for a share in the profits, or for a fixed remuneration. His function is to keep an eye on the general symmetry of the book, and to turn the actual author's amateurish sentences into respectable, flowing English. However badly the actual author writes, he should, if he wishes the best ultimate result, write out the whole book himself after discussing the outlines of it with the assistant; the assistant will then re-write it in consultation with him. The preface, if any, &c., should be done last of all. The assistant's name does not appear on the title-page.

CHAPTER X

PLAYWRITING

CHAPTER X

PLAYWRITING

Conditions of the Stage.

It is of course impossible for me, in a book of this scope and these dimensions, to deal adequately with such a complex subject as the art, craft, and business of writing for the stage. I shall pretend to do no more than offer a brief sketch of the conditions of the modern theatre, together with a few hints for the aspiring dramatist. The artistic level of the English stage is at present low. It is much higher than it was twenty years ago, but scarcely so high as it was five or six years ago. There are certainly a few talented playwrights; but there is no living acted playwright whose talent, had it been a talent for fiction, would have raised him beyond the second or third rank as a novelist. Our best plays, as works of art, are strikingly inferior to our best novels. A large section of the educated public ignores the modern English theatre as being unworthy of attention. A really fine serious modern play, dealing honestly with modern life as the best novels deal honestly with modern life, has not the slightest chance of being presented unless it happens to contain a magnificent part for an eminent player, a part such as Magda in Suderman's *Heimath*, played by Mrs. Patrick Campbell. And it may be said that no play of which the *mise-en-scène* is not luxurious and the characters not rich or titled, can get itself produced for a run under any circumstances. The playgoing public does not like artistic and truthful plays; or at any rate the modern dramatist with sufficient creative energy in him to force the public to like artistic and truthful plays has not yet come to the front. The most successful modern plays are a mixture of sweet sentimentality and ingenuous farce. The most artistic of successful plays during the last ten years have nearly all been farces. And every successful play of serious pretensions has made glaring concessions of sentimentality to the public taste.

No one in particular is to blame for this state of affairs. The standard of taste rises and falls inexplicably. The nation as a whole must blame the whole nation. The playwrights do the best they can; the managers do the best they can; and the public would be unspeakably foolish to go and see that which it did not enjoy. One of the most successful and enlightened managers in London told me once, in a burst of unwonted confidence, that throughout his management he had only produced one play which gave real satisfaction to himself. In response to my query he named a piece (not a modern one) which was decidedly a work of art. That there is a genuine desire among the best managers to produce good plays I am convinced. But the manager's first desideratum is, and ought to be, a remunerative box-office. The people who inveigh against the English stage, and suggest measures for its reform, are misguided. Nothing will reform the stage but a general upward movement of dramatic taste. When the theatrical public begins to approach the artistic level of the musical public and of the fiction-reading public, then also the theatre will begin to be reformed.

But the theatre can never offer the same

untrammelled opportunities to the creative artist as the novel. Its machinery is too vast, intricate, and subject to breakdown. The dramatist who means to gain the general ear is compelled to adapt himself to so many various conditions that he cannot hope, even under the best circumstances, to attain a free expression of his mind. He is bound to consider the salaries and idiosyncrasies of actors and actresses, the hours of dinner and of suburban trains, the specialities of theatres, the limitations of stages, the etiquette of green-rooms. These and similar founts of anxiety and trouble are eternal.

Divisions of the Theatre.

The London stage may be roughly divided into three parts. First and most opulent, the division of musical comedy. The manufacture of musical comedy is interesting and curious, but I am not aware that it has anything to do with dramatic art. A more important point is that the world of musical comedy is a self-contained world, an island cut off from the larger world of the stage. I do not think that there is any room in it for an outsider. Its gates are shut against strange faces; and indeed the capitalists of musical comedy have every reason to be content with the men they have got. The second division is that of melodrama, not on the whole a very flourishing division. The decline of melodrama was clearly shown in the transmogrification of the Adelphi Theatre a few years ago. The few successful melodramas seem now to come principally from the United States. The third (miscellaneous) division is that of comedy —a term of wide significance which includes both farces (usually called "light comedies," or "farcical comedies"), and comedies proper —and "drama," costume or otherwise. This third division alone possesses any sort of an artistic ideal. It is mainly under the control of a few actor-managers, men of some education who, while they desire money, desire more than money; and it is beyond question prepared to welcome the absolute outsider.

The Chance of Getting In.

There are eight or ten theatres in London under regular and successful managements who find the supply of suitable plays rather inadequate to the demand, and who are ready to buy suitable plays, no matter who offers them. Many times have I heard managers confess, after the event, that they had been "up a tree" for lack of a suitable play. I am acquainted with a number of instances in which first-class West End managers have bought plays from playwrights of no reputation and no experience. One manager once assured me that he attached no importance whatever to the name of the author of a play, and that, other things being equal, he preferred an unknown author, since an unknown author would be content with smaller royalties. "Your famous playwright," he added bitterly, "wants *all* the profits."

One of the most extraordinary mysteries about the modern stage is that more men are not tempted to make a bid for the splendid rewards which it showers on the successful dramatist. I have been admitted to some of the managerial secrets of a West End theatre second to none in renown, in success, and in the inclusive breadth of its répertoire. I have seen the book containing particulars of every play offered to that theatre. I was curious enough to count the number offered in the course of a year; it was just a hundred. The manager appeared to think that a hundred plays per annum was a lot, and he was astonished when I told him that in a similar period a first-class firm of publishers (with not a tenth of a theatre's notoriety) will receive upwards of a thousand manuscripts.

The aspirant who sends a manuscript to a good West End theatre may be sure that it will be considered, and that if it contains even the germ only of a possible play, he will be treated with courtesy and consideration. He may have some difficulty in recovering possession of his manuscript, owing to the unbusiness-like habits which prevail in some theatres; but pertinacity will triumph over negligence. In some other theatres he will find an official precision which equals the precision of a City merchant. The somewhat morbid conditions of stage-life have a tendency to make certain histrionic lights rather difficult to deal with; in one or two cases the difficulty is extreme and acute. But on the whole the conduct of negotiations and the transaction of business generally in the theatrical world are rendered pleasant by long traditions of courtesy and good fellowship. The very best theatres are most willing to receive the advances of a stranger.

Writing a Marketable Play.

In conceiving a play, the dramatic aspirant should consider, at the very beginning, what theatre it is likely to suit best, and he should arrange the characters so as to suit the principal regular actors and actresses at that theatre. The casting of a piece is a difficult, delicate, and extremely important business, and many a play has been refused, or has been "hung up" for years, because of the impossibility of satisfactorily casting it. He must also remember that actor-managers and leading ladies nearly always insist on "sympathetic" parts. One actor-manager declines to make love on the stage. Another declines to appear without making love. One leading lady likes to play pretty widows. Another insists on being either a pure English maiden or a newly-wed wife. These persons know what they can do with the greatest effect; they know what secures the loudest "call"; and they naturally insist on doing just that thing and no other—especially as they happen to live and flourish at a time when the drama is regarded by the public as secondary in importance to the individualities of the interpreters. To-day, the play must adapt itself to the company, and not the company to the play. Artistically, this system is entirely vicious, but there it is; and there it will be until a few dramatists of first-rate importance supervene and alter it.

The dramatic aspirant must also bear in mind that the following points are essential in a marketable play:—

(1) Plenty of contrasting action and business, and at least one big "situation" in each act.

(2) Effective "curtains" to each act.

(3) Plenty of comic relief.

(4) A luxurious environment.

(5) At least one character of great wealth, and a few titled characters if possible.

(6) Sentimentality in the love scenes, and generally throughout.

(7) A certain amount of epigram in the dialogue.

(8) No genuine realism, unless it is imme-

diately made palatable by subsequent sentimentality.

(9) A happy ending. Or at any rate a decent ending—such as the suicide of a naughty heroine.

In regard to composition, the remarks which I made about fiction apply with almost equal force to the drama. "Accurate construction" is the first and most important step in the process. The first act is seldom difficult to construct, the last act is always difficult; it is easier to propound a problem than to solve it. In playwriting the plot is everything—or nearly so. Once the plot is soundly done, the dialogue—as a dramatist phrased it to me—is "as easy as falling off a log." The aspirant must never lose sight of the fact that a play is nothing but a story told through the mouths of the people in the story. Let him insist on that truth to his unconscious self: A play is a story. A play should only contain matter which helps to tell the story, and when the aspirant ceases to tell the story in order to be funny, or to draw tears, or to convey a moral or immoral lesson, he is sinning against the canons of playwriting whether commercial or artistic.

What the public wants, and therefore what the managers want, is amusing plays, digestive plays. A moderately clever amusing play has a better chance than a very clever serious play. In this connection I will point out that the only class of modern play in which it is possible to be both quite artistic and quite marketable, is the farce.

The Curtain-Raiser.

It will be well for the aspirant to begin with a simple one-act play of three or four characters. It should "play" from twenty minutes to half an hour (between three and four thousand words of actual dialogue). It should be mildly amusing and mildly sentimental, and quite pure, because it has to appeal to the pit and gallery as distinguished from the stalls and dress-circle. The demand for curtain-raisers is not immense, but it is appreciable. When a new three or four act piece is produced at 8.30 on the first night, the probability is that after a few weeks it will be timed to begin at 8.45 or 9, and a curtain-raiser put in front of it to "strengthen the bill." Sometimes, when the success of the main piece trembles in the balance, a curtain-raiser with a star-part for the star-actor is put on and disaster averted.

One-act pieces are not strikingly remunerative, but, on the other hand, the veriest dullard could not spend more than a week in writing one. Some managers prefer to buy them outright for sums ranging from £25 to £50, and sometimes more. On the royalty system the author's fee varies from 10s. to £1 per performance. The author should always reserve the amateur rights of a curtain-raiser, and when it has been successfully produced at a West End theatre he should invite the managing director of Messrs. French, Limited (theatrical publishers, Strand), to witness it. If Messrs. French, Limited, are pleased with it, they will print it and put it in their lists for amateur dramatic societies, and collect a fee for the author of a guinea per performance (less commission). Many one-act pieces have in this manner yielded a regular annual income for considerable periods.

Curtain-raisers do not usually run as long as three or four act pieces.

Longer Plays.

When writing a full-sized play the aspirant should do a full description of the plot ("scenario") and write the first act, and should then submit this to a manager or to several managers. The manager will have before him quite sufficient material to enable him to judge whether he is likely to approve of the completed play. What managers think of first is the "idea" of the play. They do not, customarily, regard a play as an organic whole consisting of many equally important parts, but as a sort of nut with a kernel in it; that kernel is the "idea"—the salient situation. They are fascinated, not by plays, but by "ideas" for plays, by single situations, by ingenious groupings. If there is an attractive "idea" in your first act or scenario, the manager may encourage you vocally to proceed. (It is advisable to see managers the moment they evince the slightest interest in your achievements. They can almost always be seen without undue formalities, and they can always be seen by the diplomatist who is determined to see them.) If there is an exceptionally attractive idea in your first act or scenario, the manager may probably be induced to encourage you to proceed by something more valuable than words. A not unusual course is for the manager to pay £100 down on the playwright undertaking to finish the play by an agreed date, and to give the manager the option of buying the dramatic rights on agreed terms. If the manager refuses the play on its completion, he loses the £100 which he has already paid, and the playwright is £100 in pocket, with a play to sell. If the manager accepts the play on its completion, he usually pays a second £100 to seal the bargain, and the dramatic rights become his on condition that he produces the piece within an agreed period—say two years.

No manager will enter into an absolute contract to produce a play (with possible exceptions in the case of the work of supereminent playwrights). A manager will only enter into a contract either to produce within an agreed period, or, in default, to forfeit all his rights and all sums already paid. If he produces, all sums already paid are reckoned as on account of royalties. It is important that the aspirant should remember this. A contract for production does not infallibly mean production.

And in fact all managers enter into contracts about plays which they never produce. Forfeit money on non-produced plays is a regular item of managerial expenditure.

The usual royalties on a three or four act piece are as follows:—Taking the West End gross weekly receipts, week by week, the author is paid 5 per cent. on the first £750, 7½ per cent. on the next £250, and 10 per cent. on everything over £1000. Provincial rights are specially arranged for. Foreign rights are either specially arranged for or are reserved by the author. A West End theatre of average spaciousness will hold £250 per night when it is full. At the rate of six nights and one matinée per week this means a grand weekly total of possible receipts of £1750. On £1750 the author's fees would be £131, 5s. In practice, however, a theatre is seldom or never full for a week together. Some West End theatres can be run on £500 a week, or perhaps less. The author's fees on £500 would only be £25. But even at their least brilliant the profits of successful playwriting are very large in comparison with the profits of successful fiction. Sums of five, ten, and twenty thousand pounds are made from a single play in London alone. And a London success often means an American success, and an American success means profits to the English author not much less than the London profits.

In conclusion I would say that, although the supply of marketable plays is not equal to the demand, although successful managers are ready to buy plays from outsiders, although successful managers actually do buy plays from outsiders, the chances of a beginner getting a long play produced for a run in a first-rate West End theatre are extremely small.

PRINTERS' MARKS GENERALLY USED FOR CORRECTING FOR PRESS

1 THE history of the Ballantyne press is associated 2
3 with the most brilliant period of Scottish literature.
During the later years of the last, and the early part of
4 the century present, while Coleridge, Wordsworth, Bvron 4
and a host of others were making their splendid contri-
butions to English literature, there existed in Edinburgh
5 a society of ~~light bearers~~ who have become world famous. 6
Jeffrey, Cockburn, Brougham, Christopher North, Dugald
Stewart, Hogg, Horner, Abercrombie Jameson, Lockhart, 7
and many others—though, individually, some of them
8 might scarcely comparewith their Eng lish contemporaries 9
—formed a coterie which had for its nucleus the author
of his age—SIR WALTER SCOTT. The literary prestige 10
11 w/ich the northern capital acquired in the days of
12 Waverley and the "*Edinburgh Review*," has been well 13
maintained, although in these later times the great capital
of the nation absorbs her most illustrious men. It was 14
during the period referred to, and by aid of its famous 15
16 patron ~~and friend~~, that the BALLANTYNE PRESS first earned
its reputation.

17 Scott and Ballantyne were in the grammar school of 18
Kelso, and their youthful acquaintance was destined to
develop into a lifetime of business relationship and firm
19 friendship In 1790, JAMES BALLANTYNE had established 20
himself at Kelso, where he edited and printed the Mail 21
newspaper This being only a weekly publication, he be-
22 came desirus to engage in some literary enterprise which 23
might employ his press during the intervening days, and
in this he was assisted by his ~~old~~ friend and schoolfellow. 24

25 In 1799, when Scott was at Rosebank, Ballantyne begged
him to supply a few paragraphs no some legal questions of 26
the day for his newspaper. Scott complied, and, carrying 27

---

[1] Instructs that the line is not to be indented.

[2 10] Directs that the triple and double underlined words are to be made capitals and small capitals.

[3] A letter placed upside down is to be turned.

[4 25] Marks for transposition of words, sentences, and letters.

[5] Delete the scored-out word, and substitute the one written on margin.

[6] Take out the black mark between the words.

[7 12 19 27] Show the marks used for insertion of point and quotation marks.

[8] Insert a space between the words.

[9] Make close, by taking out the space.

[11] Change the wrong letter in "which."

[13] Change the underscored italic words to roman.

[14] *N.P.*—A new paragraph is to begin here.

THE history of the BALLANTYNE PRESS is associated with the most brilliant period of Scottish literature. During the later years of the last, and the early part of the present century, while Byron, Wordsworth, Coleridge, and a host of others, were making their splendid contributions to English literature, there existed in Edinburgh a society of litterateurs who have become world famous. Jeffrey, Cockburn, Brougham, Christopher North, Dugald Stewart, Hogg, Horner, Abercrombie, Jameson, Lockhart, and many others—though, individually, some of them might scarcely compare with their English contemporaries —formed a coterie which had for its nucleus the author of his age—SIR WALTER SCOTT. The literary prestige which the northern capital acquired in the days of "Waverley" and the "Edinhurgh Review" has been well maintained, although in these later times the great capital of the nation absorbs her most illustrious men.

It was during the period referred to, and by the aid of its famous patron, that the BALLANTYNE PRESS first earned its reputation. Scott and Ballantyne were, in 1783, hoys of abeut the same age at the grammar school of Kelso, and their youthful acquaintance was destined to develop into a lifetime of business relationship and firm friendship. In 1796, James Ballantyne had established himself at Kelso, where he edited and printed the *Mail* newspaper. This being only a weekly publication, he became desirous to engage in some literary enterprise which might employ his press during the intervening days, and in this he was assisted by his old friend and schoolfellow.

In 1799, when Scott was at Rosebank, Ballantyne begged him to supply a few paragraphs on some legal questions of the day for his newspaper. Scott complied: and, carrying

---

[14] [15] The first shows the method of writing in a short insertion, the second a long one.

[16] Delete the two scored-out words.

[17] *run on*—no new paragraph here.

[20] *l.-case* or *l.c.* ("lower case")—the underlined words to be altered to small letters.

[21] The word "Mail," in roman type, to be changed to italic.

[22] Insert a letter in misspelled word.

[23] Set straight the crooked lines.

[24] *stet* (Latin, "let it stand") directs that a word inadvertently struck out is to remain.

[25] *w.f.* ("wrong fount") points out that a figure or letter does not range with the others.

Observation.—Every mark made by the corrector on the page of letterpress should be supplemented by a corresponding mark on the margin. The compositor, when correcting, looks for both the *one* and the *other*.

INDEX

Index

Index

Index

THE END